THE
TWINS
OF
AUSCHWITZ

THE
TWINS
OF
AUSCHWITZ

The inspiring true story
of a young girl
surviving Mengele's hell

Eva Mozes Kor
& Lisa Rojany Buccieri

monoray

An Hachette UK Company
www.hachette.co.uk

First published in Great Britain in 2020 by Monoray, an imprint of
Octopus Publishing Group Ltd
Carmelite House
50 Victoria Embankment
London EC4Y 0DZ
www.octopusbooks.co.uk

Published in the United States as *Surviving
the Angel of Death* by Tanglewood Publishing, Inc.,
1060 N. Capitol Ave., Suite E-395, Indianapolis, IN 46204

ISBN 978-1-91318-357-8

A CIP catalogue record for this book is available from the British Library.

Printed and bound in Great Britain

10 9 8 7 6 5 4 3 2 1

CONTENTS

DEDICATION

This book is dedicated to the memory of my mother, Jaffa Mozes, my father, Alexander Mozes, my sisters, Edit and Aliz, and my twin sister, Miriam Mozes Zeiger. I also dedicate this book to the children who survived the camp, and to all the children in the world who have survived neglect and abuse, for I wish to honor their struggle in overcoming the trauma of losing their childhoods, their families, and the feeling that they belong to a family. Last, but not least, this book is dedicated in honor of my son, Alex Kor, and my daughter, Rina Kor, who are my joy, pride, and challenge.

—*EMK*

To Olivia, Chloe, and Genevieve: the reasons for everything. And to my sister, Amanda, for saving my life.

—*LRB*

PROLOGUE

The doors of the train car were thrown all the way open for the first time in many days, the light of day shining upon us like a blessing. Dozens of Jewish people had been crammed into that tiny cattle car as it rattled through the countryside, taking us farther and farther away from our home in Romania. Desperate, people pushed their way out.

I held tightly to my twin sister's hand as we were shoved onto the platform, not sure whether to be glad for our release or afraid of what was coming. The early-morning air was chilly, a cold wind nipping at our bare legs through the thin fabric of our matching burgundy dresses.

I could tell at once that it was very early morning, the sun barely making its way above the horizon.

Everywhere I looked there were tall, sharp, barbed-wire fences. High guard towers with SS patrols, *Schutzstaffel* in German, leaned out, aiming their guns at us. Guard dogs held by other SS soldiers pulled against leashes, barking and growling like a rabid dog I had once seen on the farm, their lips foaming, their teeth flashing white and pointy. I could feel my heart pounding.

My sister's palm clenched sweaty and warm onto my own. My mother and father and our two older sisters, Edit and Aliz, were standing right next to us when I heard my mother's loud whisper to my father.

"Auschwitz? It's Auschwitz? What is this place? It's not Hungary?"

"We are in Germany," came the reply.

We had crossed over the border into German territory. In actuality, we were in Poland, but the Germans had taken over Poland. Germany's Poland was where all the extermination camps were. We had not been taken to a Hungarian labor camp to work but to a Nazi extermination camp to die. Before we had time to digest this news, I felt my shoulder being pushed to one side of the platform.

"*Schnell! Schnell!*" Quick! Quick! SS guards ordered the remaining prisoners from the cattle car out onto the large platform.

Miriam pulled herself closer to me as we were jostled about. The weak daylight was blocked and unblocked as taller people were first jammed up next to us, then pulled away by the guards to one side or the other. It looked like they were choosing some of us prisoners for one thing and some for another. But for what?

That's when the sounds around us began escalating. The Nazi guards grabbed more people, pulling them to the right or to the left on the selection platform. Dogs were snarling and barking. The people from the cattle car started crying, yelling, screaming all at once; everyone was looking for family members as they were torn away from one another. Men were separated from women, children from parents. The morning erupted into pure pandemonium. Everything started moving faster and faster around us. It was bedlam.

"*Zwillinge! Zwillinge!*" Twins! Twins! Within seconds,

a guard who had been hurrying by stopped short in front of us. He stared at Miriam and me in our matching clothes.

"Are they twins?" he asked Mama.

She hesitated. "Is that good?"

"Yes," said the guard.

"They are twins," replied Mama.

Without a word, he grabbed Miriam and me and tore us away from Mama.

"No!"

"Mama! Mama! No!"

Miriam and I screamed and cried, reaching out for our mother, who, in turn, was struggling to follow us with her arms outstretched, a guard holding her back. He threw her roughly to the other side of the platform.

We shrieked. We cried. We pleaded, our voices lost among the chaos and noise and despair. But no matter how much we cried or how loud we screamed, it did not matter. Because of those matching burgundy dresses, because we were identical twins so easily spotted in the crowd of grimy, exhausted Jewish prisoners, Miriam

4

and I had been chosen. Soon we would come face to face with Josef Mengele, the Nazi doctor known as the Angel of Death. It was he who selected those on the platform who were to live and those who would die. But we did not know that yet. All we knew was that we were abruptly alone. We were only ten years old.

And we never saw Papa, Mama, Edit, or Aliz again.

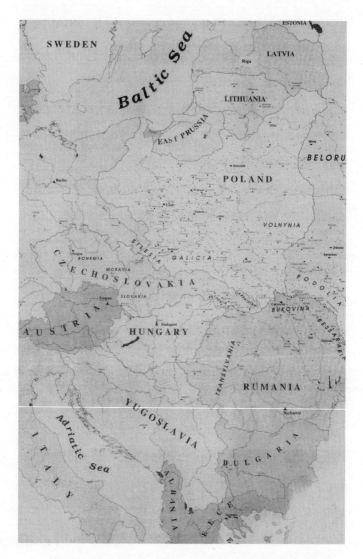

Eastern Europe at the beginning of World War II

CHAPTER ONE

Miriam and I were identical twins, the youngest of four sisters. To hear my older sisters grudgingly tell the story of our birth, you would have known immediately that we two were the darlings of the family. What is sweeter or cuter than identical twin girls?

We were born on January 31, 1934, in the village of Portz in Transylvania, Romania, which is near the border of Hungary. From the time we were babies, our mother loved to dress us in the same clothes, putting huge bows in our hair so people would know right away that we little people were twins. She even seated us on the windowsill of our home; passersby thought we were precious dolls, not even real people.

We looked so much alike that she had to put tags on us to tell us apart. Aunts, uncles, and cousins visiting our farm liked to play guessing games with us, trying to divine who was who. "Which one is Miriam? Which one is Eva?" a puzzled uncle would muse with a twinkle in his eye. My mother would smile proudly at her perfect little dolls, and my two older sisters would probably groan. Regardless, most people guessed wrong. When we were older and in school, we would use our identical twinship to trick people, which for us could be so much fun. And we took advantage of how precious and unique we were whenever we could.

Although Papa was strict and admonished us and our mother about the perils of excessive vanity, emphasizing that even the Bible warned against it, Mama particularly cared about our appearance. She had our clothes custom-made just for us, like rich people do today with fashion designers. She would order material from the city, and when it arrived, she would take Miriam and me and our two older sisters, Edit and Aliz, to a seamstress in the nearby village of Szeplak. At her house, we girls were permitted to hungrily peruse magazines featuring models wearing the latest styles. But our mother made

Eva and Miriam Mozes, 1935

Eva's parents, Alexander and Jaffa Mozes

the final decision on the cut and color of our dresses, for in those days girls always wore dresses, never pants or overalls like boys. And always our mother chose burgundy, powder blue, and pink for Miriam and me. After we were measured, we would set a date for a fitting, and when we returned, the seamstress had the dresses ready for us to try on. The styles and colors of the dresses were always identical, two pieces made into one perfect, matching pair.

Other people may have been baffled by our identical twinship, but our father could tell Miriam and me apart by our personalities. By the way I carried my body, a gesture I would make, or the second I opened my mouth to speak, it was clear to him who was who. Although my sister had been born first, I was the leader. I was also outspoken. Any time we needed to ask Papa for something, my oldest sister Edit would encourage me to be the one to approach him.

My father, a religious Jew, had always wanted a boy, because at that time only a son could participate in public worship and say *Kaddish*, the Jewish mourner's prayer, upon someone's death. But Papa had no son, only my sisters and me. Since I was the younger of the twins and his last child, he often looked at me and said, "You should have been a boy." I think he meant to say that I was his last chance at getting a boy. My personality just cemented it: I was strong and brave and more outspoken—just like he must have imagined a son of his might have been.

This stronger personality of mine, while setting me apart, also had its downside. It seemed to me that my father believed that everything about me was wrong; nothing I did seemed to please him. Many a time we would argue and debate, me not willing to give in. It was not enough of an answer for me that my father was right just because he was a man and my father and the head of the household. So we always seemed to be disagreeing, Papa and I.

I definitely got more attention from him than Miriam or my other sisters, but it was not always the kind of attention I wanted. I never learned to skirt the edge of the truth with little white lies, so I was always in trouble. I can recall tiptoeing around the house to avoid my father sometimes, as I am sure he often tired of me and my big mouth.

Looking back, however, I realize that my battles with Papa toughened me up, made me even stronger. I learned to outsmart authority. These battles with my father unwittingly prepared me for what was to come.

My mother was very different from my father. She was quite educated for a woman of those times, because not all women got to go to school. Especially among religious Jews in those days, girls and women were mostly expected to take care of the home and the family, while the education and studying was reserved for the boys. And while my mother made sure that we learned to read, write, and do math, and study history and languages, she also taught us to care for others in our community.

We were the only Jewish family in Portz, our village, and were friendly with everyone. My mother heard all the town news and often assisted our neighbors, especially young pregnant mothers in times of need.

She would take them noodles or cake, help them with the household if they were sick, give them advice on raising children, and read them instructions or letters from other family members. She taught me and my sisters to follow in her lead, serving those less fortunate, especially since we were better off than many other people in our small farming village.

Yet almost from the time we were born, anti-Semitism pervaded our country of Romania. That means that most of the people around us did not like Jewish people just because they were Jewish. We children were never aware of the anti-Semitism until 1940, when the Hungarian army came.

My father once told us of an anti-Semitic incident that happened to him in 1935 when Miriam and I were just one year old. In that year, the Iron Guard—a violent anti-Semitic political party that controlled the village offices, the police, and the newspapers—stirred up hatred against Jews by making up false stories about how evil Jewish people were, and how Jews wanted to cheat everyone else and take over the world. My father and his brother Aaron were thrown into jail by the Romanian Iron Guard on fake charges of not paying taxes. But it was all a lie; they had always paid their taxes. They were singled out and arrested just because they were Jewish.

Papa told us that when he and Uncle Aaron got out of jail, they decided to go to Palestine to see if they could make a living there. Palestine, at the time, was an area of land in the Middle East where the Jewish people lived before their exile during the time of the Roman Empire; especially during periods of persecution, it was always thought of as a homeland by many Jews. A part of Palestine had been set aside for Jewish immigration early in the twentieth century, and it eventually became the independent state of Israel in 1948.

My father and Uncle Aaron stayed in Palestine a few months and then came back to Romania. Upon their return, Uncle Aaron and his wife sold all their land and possessions and planned to emigrate, or move.

Papa urged Mama to leave and settle in Palestine, too. "It's good there," he said. "The country is warm. There are plenty of jobs."

"No," she protested. "I can't move with four small children."

"We need to leave now, before it gets worse here for us," urged my father, who was worried about the news he was hearing of increasing persecution of the Jews all over the country and Europe.

"What would I do there? How would we manage? I have no desire to live in the desert," said my mother. And like mothers sometimes do, she put her foot down and refused to go. I have often wondered what our lives would have been like had she relented.

In our little village in Romania, we lived in a nice house on a vast farm. We had thousands of acres of crops—wheat, corn, beans, and potatoes. We had cows and sheep, from which we produced cheese and milk. We had a large vineyard and produced wine. We had acres of orchards, giving us apples, plums, peaches, and juicy cherries in three colors: red, black, and white. In the summer, those cherries became our beautiful earrings when we pretended we were fancy, dressed-up ladies. Mama also loved her flower garden in front of the

Portz, Transylvania

Top row (l to r): Aliz, Papa, Edit, and friend Luci
Middle: Eva, Mama, Miriam. Bottom: cousin Shmulik

house and her vegetable garden in back, and her cows, chickens, and geese.

But what concerned her most was leaving behind her own mother. We children loved to visit Grandma and Grandpa Hersh. And my mother, as an only daughter, felt responsible for taking care of Grandma Hersh, who was not in the best of health and often needed Mama to look after her.

"Besides, we are safe here," said my mother. She really believed that the rumors of Jews being persecuted by the Germans and their new head of state, Adolf Hitler, were just that: rumors. She saw no need to flee to Palestine or America, places of safety for Jewish people like us. So we stayed in Portz.

Portz, a largely Christian village of one hundred families, had a minister. The minister's daughter, Luci, was our best friend; both Miriam and I loved playing with her. In the summer we climbed trees in the orchard, read stories, and put on plays in a little theater we made by stringing up a sheet between two trees. In the winter we even helped Luci decorate her Christmas tree—we did not tell our father because he would not have approved.

Though rumors of Jews being deported to labor camps began to spread here and there, Mama did not believe we were in danger. Even when we heard of the new ghettos— restricted areas of European towns where Jews were forced to live so they could be controlled in squalor and poverty— we did not believe we were really in any danger. Even when Jews were stripped of all possessions, all freedoms, sent away to labor camps and driven to work for no pay like slaves, we did not think it could happen to us. We never thought they would come to our tiny village.

One of my early memories is of the men of a Jewish labor camp from Budapest who came through our village. The Hungarian government would bring these slave laborers out of the camp to work on the railroads; when the work was completed, the laborers were taken back to the labor camp. While working on the railroad, they had nowhere to stay at night, so my father let them all sleep in our barn. Sometimes their wives would come to visit and stay in our house. In return, the women brought us lots of toys and, more importantly, lots of books from the city. We children spent hours lost in the worlds of those books. I could finish a book in a day. Because of them, I developed a love of reading at a young age.

As I understood only later from my reading, Adolf Hitler had come to power in Germany as the head of the Nazi Party in 1933. Hitler hated Jews as much as the Romanian Iron Guard did, and leaders of the anti-Semitic and racist parties became allies, joining together in their hatred and their designs to rule all of Europe. Then, in September 1939, World War II began when German Nazi troops invaded Poland. The Hungarians, under the leadership of Miklós Horthy, also trusted Hitler and became allies. All this began to happen around us, but still far enough away from us that only Papa fretted about our safety.

But in the summer of 1940, when Miriam and I were six years old, things changed. Hitler gave the northern part of Transylvania to Hungary. At that time the population in Transylvania, the larger area surrounding our village, was half-Hungarian, half-Romanian. But everyone in our village was Romanian. Rumors spread that the Hungarian army would kill Jews and Romanians and set our village on fire. Even as a six-year-old child, I knew we were in danger.

Miriam, the quieter of the two of us, felt my anxiety, must have seen it on my face and in my body language. But she never complained; it was not her nature.

One day Hungarian soldiers marched into our village, the commanding officer leading the troops in a long, shiny black car. It was impressive, as it was intended to be. We villagers were to take note: The armies were now in power, so we were to welcome them! We heard the soldiers singing, "We are Horthy's soldiers, the best-looking soldiers in the world."

That night, my mother and father allowed the soldiers to camp in our yard; the commanding officer slept in our guest room. Mama treated the officers like company: She baked her best torte and invited the officers to dine with our family. I remember that there was much conversation about good food, and Miriam and I were excited to sit at the table with these important men in uniform. It was a pleasant evening, and the officers praised Mama's cooking and baking. Before they went to sleep, they kissed her hand as they thanked her, a courtly habit of many European and Hungarian men of the time. Early the next morning they left, and our parents seemed to be reassured.

"See?" said Mama. "There is no truth to the talk that they are killing the Jews. They are real gentlemen."

"Why would people tell such stories?" Papa asked, not expecting an answer, much less disagreement from my mother or anyone else in the family. "You're right. Nazis will never come to a small village like ours," he concluded. This we were to take as fact. Papa had said it.

Yet late at night, behind closed doors, our parents listened to a battery-operated radio. They spoke to each other in Yiddish, a language none of us girls understood, as they discussed the news. What was it they were hearing that could be so secret? That could make them try to hide it from us girls?

I pressed my ear against the door and eavesdropped, trying to hear what was happening. "Who is Hitler?" I asked when they came out.

Mama brushed off our questions with blithe reassurances: "You don't need to worry about anything. Everything will be fine." But we had overheard some of the radio broadcasts with Hitler yelling about killing all the Jews. As if we were bugs! We *felt* there was trouble, no matter how much our parents tried to reassure us otherwise. And because of their secretive behavior, even Miriam became anxious. We were always worried, even as young children. There was a disquiet about the unspoken, the undiscussed.

That autumn, in 1940, Miriam and I started school. Unlike elementary schools today, our schoolhouse had children from first grade to the fourth grade in one room. Miriam and I were the only Jews. We were also the only twins. Every day we wore matching outfits to school and the same color ribbons tied at the ends of our long braids. Like our family had before them, our new classmates enjoyed figuring out which twin was which.

We also discovered we had two new Hungarian teachers at school who had been brought in from the city by the Nazis. To my surprise, they brought with them books containing slurs against Jews. The books also showed cartoon caricatures depicting Jews as clowns with big noses and bulging bellies. And marvel of marvels, for the first time, we saw "jumping pictures" projected on the wall—which is what we called early motion pictures because we did not know what a film was. I clearly remember watching the short film called "How to Catch and Kill a Jew." These propaganda films, something like today's commercials but filled with hatred, were shown before feature films in the theaters in cities. Imagine watching instructions on how to kill Jews right before a Pixar movie!

Watching the hate movie and reading these racist books inflamed the other students. Our friends, or other children who had been friends, started calling Miriam and me names like "dirty, smelly Jews." Their name-calling really made me angry. Who were they to call us dirty? I knew I was as clean as, if not cleaner than, any of them! Kids began to spit at us and beat us up at every opportunity. One day, our math book contained this problem: "If you had five Jews, and you killed three Jews, how many Jews would be left?"

Upset and frightened, Miriam and I ran home crying. Our clothes were filthy from being pushed into the dirt once again, and our dusty faces were streaked with tears. "Children, I'm so sorry," Mama said, hugging and kissing us, "but there is nothing we can do. Don't worry! Just be good girls. Say your prayers, do your chores around the farm, and study your reading."

One day at school in 1941 some boys played a trick on the teacher when her back was turned. They placed birds' eggs on her chair. The entire class knew they were there, but no one said a word. We all held our breath as she turned around and sat down. Of course, the second her behind hit the chair, the eggs broke, spattering on her new dress.

"The dirty Jews did it!" stated one of the boys in our class matter-of-factly.

"Did you?" asked the teacher, looking at Miriam and me.

"No, Madame Teacher, no!" We were horrified. We had never misbehaved like that or played a trick on a teacher. We would never have heard the end of it from our parents had we dared! And we loved school and loved learning.

And then it happened. "Yes, they did!" screamed the other children. "They did it! We saw them!" It was as if they had all made a secret pact behind our backs beforehand, and this was the result.

Miriam and I protested, but to no avail. We were Jews, and we were guilty.

Without asking more questions, the teacher called us up to the front of the class for our punishment. She threw dry corn kernels onto the floor. "Kneel!" she demanded, pointing to us. For an hour, she made us kneel on those corn kernels in front of the class. The hard kernels dug into the flesh of our bare knees. But that was not what really wounded us the most. What hurt most were our classmates taunting us, leering at us, making ugly, smirking faces at us. Miriam and I were as shocked as we were hurt.

When we came home and told our mother, crying and hugging us, she said, "Children, I am sorry. We are Jews, and we just have to take it. There is nothing we can do." Her words made me angrier than the teacher's punishment. I wanted to hit someone myself, pound something hard like those kernels into dry corn dust. How could Mama's words be true?

When Papa came in from farming at the end of the day and heard what had happened to us, his attitude was like Mama's. "For two thousand years the Jews have believed that if they tried to get along, they would survive," he said. "We must obey tradition. Just try to get along." Papa reasoned that since we lived so far out in the middle of nowhere, the Nazis would not bother to come take us away.

In the afternoon and evenings, the disturbances continued. Teenage boys who belonged to the Hungarian Nazi Party, but who were not yet eighteen years old—the age at which they could begin to serve in the military—often surrounded our house and shouted obscenities at us for hours. "Dirty Jews!" they yelled. "Crazy pigs!" They threw tomatoes or rocks that smashed right through our windows. Other villagers joined in. Sometimes this would go on for three entire days with us unable to leave the house.

"Papa," I called, "please go out and make them stop!" I wanted him to *do* something!

"Eva, there is nothing we can do about it. So just learn to take it."

I could not have known it at the time, but Mama and Papa must have felt that if they tried to stop these juvenile delinquents or fight back, they would be arrested and taken away from us. At least we were all still together as a family.

Miriam and I huddled together in our bed, frightened. Our sisters stayed away from the windows. I know they were scared as well. Conditions grew increasingly worse. In June 1941, Hungary entered World War II as an ally, or partner in war, of Jew-hating Adolf Hitler and Germany, his country. Jews in other places in Europe were forced to wear a yellow Star of David—the Jewish star—on the outside of their clothing or on their jackets to let everyone know that they were Jewish. We did not have to wear the yellow star, but everyone knew that we were Jewish. We were increasingly isolated in our village.

Unlike many Jewish children in Europe, Miriam and I were still allowed to attend school with other non-Jewish children, although it was progressively more difficult for us there, as the teasing and taunting did not stop. Our lucky older sisters, Edit and Aliz, were tutored in German, art, music, drawing, math, and history—all the subjects required in high school—by a Jewish teacher who lived with us at home.

As the light of autumn darkened into early winter, the days became shorter and our lives became more constricted. We did not venture to play outside or go into the village as much as we used to. Our parents never let on what they were feeling, but Miriam and I grew more and more afraid.

Then one night in late September 1943, Mama and Papa shook us awake. "Eva! Miriam!" they hissed urgently. "Get dressed! Put on your warm clothes, as many as you can get on, with your jackets and your boots. Do *not* light that candle! It has to stay dark. And be very, very quiet."

"Wha-what are we doing?" I asked sleepily. "Just do as you're told!" murmured Papa.

We piled on our warm clothing and went into the kitchen. By the light of the glowing embers in the fireplace, we saw our older sisters standing there. They were bundled up as well, their faces like stones in the shadows.

Papa gathered the four of us girls together and whispered, "Children, the time has come when we must leave. We are going to try to get over the border to the non-Hungarian side of Romania where we will be safe. Follow us and remember: no noise."

Single file, with Papa in the lead and Mama at the rear, we slipped out of the house into the darkness. Outside it was cold and windy. But at the time I had only one thought: We were in trouble, big trouble. And we were running away.

Silently we walked, one behind the other, to the back gate of our property at the edge of the orchard.

Just beyond the gate lay the railroad tracks. No trains passed at night. It was silent except for the sounds of the crickets and the occasional call of a night bird. If we were to walk along the tracks for an hour or so, we knew we would arrive at the safe part of Romania. When Papa reached the gate at the edge of our property, he leaned over to unlatch it and pushed it open.

"Stop!" shouted a voice. "If you take another step, I'll shoot!"

A Hungarian Nazi youth pointed a gun at us. A group of teenage boys wearing Hungarian Nazi armbands with swastikas and khaki caps had been guarding our farm, stationed there to make sure we did not get away. How long they had been there was anyone's guess.

We were only six Jews. How could we be so important? I clutched Miriam's hand, not daring to look directly at them, but sneaking sideways glimpses at the soldiers. Papa closed the gate, and the boys marched us right back to our house.

Our only chance of escape had just vanished.

CHAPTER TWO

On January 31, 1944, Miriam and I would turn ten years old. On family birthdays, Mama had always baked a cake and made the day a fun and festive occasion. But Miriam and I never got to celebrate our tenth birthday. Mama was too sick. Since October, just after the teenage Nazis had prevented our escape, she had been ill with typhoid fever and had stayed in bed all winter. In those days there were no simple medicines to ease the pains of fever and illness like there are today in every pharmacy. We worried about her and whether she would get better. Our mother had always been so strong and healthy.

A Jewish lady from a nearby village came to live with us to take care of our mother and run the house. Edit, Aliz, Miriam, and I helped by doing more than our usual share of chores on the farm. The Nazis and the Hungarian authorities were watching us, but we were never under house arrest or forbidden from leaving our home. For the moment, we seemed safe. We even continued to attend school, except on the rare days the Nazis did not allow us to go. On those days we were tutored at home like our older sisters.

Our relative freedom came to an abrupt end one morning in March, that year we turned ten. Two Hungarian *gendarmes*, or policemen, arrived in our front yard. Soon they were pounding on the door.

"Get your belongings! Gather them up. You are going to be moved to a transportation center." This was not a request; it was a command. "You have two hours to pack."

Mama barely had the strength to get out of bed. Papa and our older sisters bundled up food, bedding, clothing—all the necessities they could think of. Miriam and I wore matching dresses and took two other sets of identical clothes.

As the policemen marched us out of our home, everyone in Portz watched us leave on the one road that ran through the village. Neighbors came out of their farmhouses and lined the road. Our classmates from school just stared. No one tried to stop the *gendarmes* from taking us away. No one said a word.

I was not surprised. Once word got around that we had tried to leave in the middle of the night, conditions had continued to get worse; the harassment from the villagers and their children had grown uglier and more frequent.

Even Luci, Miriam's and my best friend, stood very still, her eyes not meeting ours as we approached her house. She did not say she was sorry nor give us anything to remember her by to take on our journey. Just before we passed her house, I glanced at her. She looked down. In silence we left the home we had always known.

We were bundled into a horse-drawn, covered wagon. The policemen took us to a town called Șimleu Silvaniei, about a five-hour ride away. Once there, we were forced to stay in a ghetto with more than seven thousand other Jews from our Romanian area of Transylvania. Miriam and I had never seen so many people. To us, one hundred people—the number of neighbors in our village—was a crowd. Seven thousand people—all of them Jews!—were more than we had ever seen at one time in our entire lives.

We later learned that Reinhard Heydrich, chief of the Third Reich Security Service, the *Sicherheitsdienst*, had issued an official order: All Jews in Nazi-occupied areas were to be moved to special places set aside for them; these special places were called ghettos. We had not heard about these ghettos before. Ghettos were areas enclosed by fences, walls, or barbed wire and were set up in the most run-down sections of cities or the poorest parts of the countryside. Jews were forbidden to leave without a special permit, upon penalty of death.

Our ghetto was located in a field enclosed by a barbed-wire fence that looked as though it had been quickly built. The Barcău (Berretyo) River ran through the middle of the field. The only building was an abandoned brick factory, which the commandant, or main security officer, occupied as his headquarters. There were no tents or cabins or other structures in which Jews could take shelter or sleep. The commandant said that we would soon be taken to work in labor camps in Hungary and would remain there until the end of the war. "No harm will come to you," he promised.

Miriam and I helped Papa and our older sisters build a tent on the damp ground out of the sheets and blankets we had brought. We struggled and huffed while the ghetto commandant strode back and forth with his hands on his hips shouting, "Isn't it nice that I get to see the children of Israel living in tents like in the days of Moses?" He laughed uproariously as if he had told himself the funniest joke on earth.

Our entire family stayed in the same tent. Every time the sky darkened and it began to rain, the commandant barked through a loudspeaker, "Take down the tents! I want them to be built now on the *other* side." There was no reason for this except simple cruelty. By the time we took down our tents, crossed the bridge, and set up our shelter again in the mud, we were soaked.

Mama was still very weak from her illness, and living

THE TWINS OF AUSCHWITZ

outdoors in the rain and cold just made her worse. At night Miriam and I slept close together, our small bodies giving each other warmth and comfort.

During our stay, the head of each family was taken to the headquarters for interrogation. One day, German guards came for Papa and took him away for questioning. They believed my parents were hiding gold and silver or had concealed valuables at our farm; they wanted to know exactly where. But Papa was a farmer and his only riches were his land and the crops he produced. He told the guards he had no silver except our Shabbat, or Sabbath, candlesticks. Four or five hours later they carried him back to our tent on a stretcher. He was covered with whip marks, oozing blood. They had burned his fingernails and toenails with the flame of candles. It took him many days to recover.

Miriam and I felt helpless. We were still children and expected our parents to take care of us. But there was nothing they could do to make it better for us. And there was nothing we could do for Papa.

Our older sister Edit took charge of the cooking. We

had been told to bring two weeks' worth of food when we came, but Mama had us girls bring everything we could carry— beans, bread, and noodles. As the weeks went by, we rationed our food and ate beans once a day. Sometimes non-Jewish people came to the edge of the ghetto and threw in food and other supplies, but I do not remember if we ever got any of that to eat.

Finally, Mama had realized just how bad things really were for our family. Miriam and I complained about sleeping on the wet ground and about that gnawing ache in our tummies all the time, but Mama could not help us as she used to do. She sat on the ground, shaking her head over and over again. "It's all my fault," she said. "We should have gone to Palestine." Her eyes, sunken by her illness and with dark circles under them from lack of proper sleep, showed that she was haunted by her decision not to flee to Palestine with Uncle Aaron when they had the chance. Now, trapped in the squalor and deprivation of the ghetto, she grew increasingly withdrawn and depressed.

On a morning in May 1944, German guards told us

we were going to a labor camp, which they said was in Hungary. "This is for your own protection. If you work you will live," they said. "Your families will stay together." We had heard rumors circulating among the grown-ups in the ghettos that Jews sent to Germany would be killed. So we thought that if we stayed in Hungary, we would be all right, we would be safe.

The guards told us to leave our belongings, that everything we would need would be at the labor camp. Nevertheless, Mama and our older sisters took a few valuables from our tent. Papa carried his prayer book. Miriam and I put on our matching burgundy dresses.

The guards marched us to the train tracks and herded us into cattle cars, pushing and shoving until one car was packed with eighty to one hundred people. The guards made Papa responsible for our car. Papa was told that if anyone escaped, he would be shot. The doors were slammed shut and sealed with a metal bar that slid into two handles. Barbed wire covered four small, high-up windows, two on each side. How could anyone escape?

Miriam and I pressed close together. There was no

room to sit or lie down, not even for young children like us. Even though I was just a little girl, I could sense that something awful was about to happen. Just seeing our parents so powerless, parents that I had always seen as our protectors no longer able to protect our family, had turned any sense of safety I had completely upside down.

For days, our train rushed along the tracks, the endless sound of the clacking interrupted only by an occasional hoot of the train's horn. Not only did we have no place to sit or lie down, we had no food or water, and no bathrooms. I remember being very thirsty, my mouth pasty and dry.

When the train stopped for refueling on the first day, Papa asked the guard for water. The guard demanded five gold watches in exchange. The grown-ups gathered the watches and handed them over. Then the guard tossed a bucketful of water toward the barbed-wired window. Water splashed in uselessly. I don't remember anyone getting any. I may have had a drop or two, but that did not begin to quench my thirst. The second day, the train stopped again, and the same thing happened with the water.

At the end of the third day, the cattle car stopped, and Papa, speaking Hungarian, asked a guard for water. Someone answered in German, *"Was? Was?"* What? What? He had not understood Papa.

Then it hit us: We were not in Hungary anymore. We had crossed the border into Poland, now German territory. A feeling of horror took hold of us. Up until then, there was hope. Everybody, including me, had understood that as long as we stayed in Hungary, there was some chance that we would go to a labor camp to work. Everyone knew by now that Germans and Germany meant death to Jews. Many people started praying. The cattle car filled with the sound of adults barely stifling their crying, children feeding off their exposed despair. Here and there someone attempted to chant the *Shema*, the Hebrew prayer to God to hear us, to save us.

The train began moving again. Miriam and I were quiet as it gathered speed, going faster and faster. We had gone three days without food or water.

On the fourth day, the train stopped. Papa called out again to the guard for water. No one answered.

We realized we must have arrived at our destination. I stood on tiptoes to look through the window. The sky was dark. We heard lots of German voices yelling orders outside for an hour or two. The doors stayed closed.

Dawn finally came, time for Papa to say his morning prayers. He took out his prayer book and tried to figure out which direction was east, because Jewish people pray to the direction of Israel, which is in the Middle East. I wondered how he could pray at a time like this.

"Papa," I said, "we don't know where we are. They have lied to us. We are not at a work camp."

"Eva, we must pray to God for mercy," said Papa. "Come to me." He pulled our family into a corner of the cattle car. Miriam and I squeezed close to him, and our sisters and Mama followed. We listened quietly to our father as he spoke. "Promise me that if any of you survives this terrible war, you will go to Palestine where your uncle Aaron lives and where Jews can live in peace."

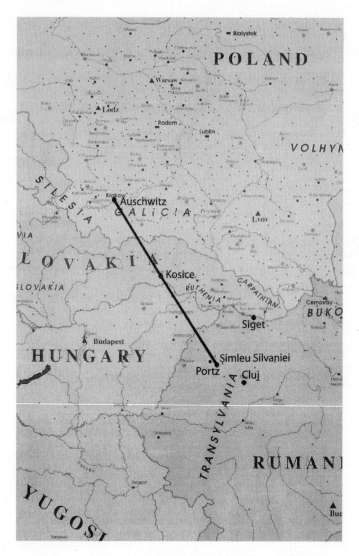

Eva's journey

He had never spoken to us girls like this before, with respect, as though we were adults. Miriam and I and our older sisters solemnly agreed.

Papa began his morning prayers.

Outside I could hear German voices yelling orders. Dogs barked at us from every direction. The doors of the cattle car screeched open. SS guards ordered everybody out.

"*Schnell! Schnell!*" Quick! Quick!

I saw tall barbed-wire fences, cement guard towers everywhere. Soldiers were hanging out of them with the barrels of their guns pointed at us. I have no idea how we got from the cattle car to the selection platform. Miriam and I may have jumped or stepped down a wooden ramp. But pretty soon we were standing on the platform in utter terror, two ten-year-olds in matching burgundy dresses.

CHAPTER THREE

Mama grabbed Miriam and me by our hands. We lined up, side by side, on the concrete platform. The smell hit me: a foul odor I had never ever smelled before. It reminded me of burned chicken feathers. At home on the farm, after plucking the chickens, we would singe off the last little feathers over a flame to clean it. But here the stink was overpowering. It was as if you walked through it, around in it. It was everywhere and inescapable. I did not find out right away what the smell really was.

This place was confusing and noisy. People were yelling. There were screams.

Confusion.

Desperation.

Barking.

Orders.

Crying, crying, crying. The crying of children for parents. The crying of parents for their babies. The crying of people confused and bewildered. The crying of people who saw with certainty that their nightmares had come true. All together, the cries resounded with the ultimate and most unimaginable pain of human loss, emotional grief, and suffering.

I felt as though I was watching things happen to someone else. Here and there I glimpsed layers of barbed-wire fences, bright klieg lights, and rows of buildings. The SS guards strode among the groups of people, as if searching for something.

Suddenly I felt like I had landed in my body again. I looked around, and I felt Miriam's quaking frame next to mine. But where was Papa? And where were my older sisters, Edit and Aliz? I searched desperately, holding tightly to my mother's and my twin's hands in a death grip. I could not find the rest of my family. After four days of such close proximity to my older sisters and Papa, in my bewilderment and confusion I had lost them.

The Auschwitz selection platform

Entrance to Auschwitz. The sign is in German and translates to: "Work makes you free."

I never saw them again.

I held tightly to Mama's hand. An SS guard rushed by. He was calling out in German, "*Zwillinge! Zwillinge!*" Twins! Twins! He barreled past us, then stopped short, whirled around, and came back. He stood in front of us. His eyes traveled back and forth from Miriam's face to mine, up and down our matching burgundy dresses.

"Are they twins?" he asked Mama.

She hesitated. "Is that good?"

"Yes," said the guard.

"They are twins," replied Mama.

Without one word, he grabbed Miriam and me, tearing us away from Mama.

We screamed and cried as we were dragged away. We begged him to let us stay with her. The German guard paid no attention to our pleas. He pulled us across the railroad tracks, away from the selection platform. I turned my head and saw my mother, desperate, her arms outstretched toward us, wailing. A soldier grabbed her and threw her in another direction. My mama disappeared into the crowd.

After that, everything happened quickly, so quickly. Guards separated people on the selection platform into groups. One group had young men and women. In another, children and older people. Miriam and I held on to each other as we were brought to join a group of thirteen sets of twins who had come from our train transport: twenty-six children, all frightened and confused.

A guard brought a mother and her twins to stand with our group. I recognized her! It was Mrs. Csengeri, wife of the storekeeper in Șimleu Silvaniei, the town near our village. Her twin daughters were eight years old, and when we shopped at her store, she and Mama liked to talk about the problems of raising twins. She and her girls stayed with our group. Why had the guards let their mother come with them and not ours with us? I did not have time to ponder the question much before things started happening again.

After half an hour, an SS guard led us to a big building near the barbed-wire fence. As soon as we entered the building, we were ordered to undress. I felt numb again, not part of my own body. This was all a nightmare, right? It would end the second I opened my eyes, and Mama would be there to comfort me, right? But I was not dreaming.

All of us were given short haircuts. The barber explained that twins received privileged treatment: We were allowed to keep some hair. Luckily, I had learned some German, so I could understand what was being said on a basic level. As I watched our long braids fall to the floor, I did not feel so very privileged.

Next, we took showers. Our clothes had been fumigated with some sort of anti-lice chemical and were returned to us. Wearing our own clothes was another "privilege" we twins got that other prisoners did not. Miriam and I put on our dresses, but now each had a big red cross painted on the back. I instantly hated that red cross on my dress. Wearing the dress did not feel like a privilege. I knew that like the yellow star they forced Jews to wear in the ghettos, the Nazis were using that red cross to mark us so that we could not escape.

Right then and there, I decided not to do anything

the guards asked me to do. I would give them as much trouble as possible. In the processing center, prisoners' arms were being tattooed. We watched as the prisoners went up one after another, were told to hold out their arms, and had their arms pinned down while the instrument seared numbers into their flesh with acute pain.

Not me. I was not going to be a sheep anymore. When my turn came, I struggled and kicked. The SS guard grabbed my arm. The feel of his grip twisting my skin dissolved my resolve. "I want my mama!" I screamed.

"Hold still!" ordered the guard.

I bit his arm. "Bring back my mama!"

"We will let you see her tomorrow."

I knew he was lying. They had just torn us away from Mama, so why would they reunite us the next day? Four people had to hold me down while they heated the point of a pen-like gadget over an open flame and dipped it into blue ink. Then they held the hot pen to my flesh and began to burn my number into the outer part of my left arm: A-7063.

Auschwitz

Inside the camp

"Stop!" I yelled. "That hurts!"

I squirmed and wriggled so much that they could not hold me completely still. Because of my struggling, the numbers on my arm were blurred.

Next, they tattooed Miriam. She did not struggle like I had. Her number was A-7064. All the writing on her arm was clear.

Our arms felt painful and swollen as we were marched across the camp to our barracks, where we would reside. Along the way I saw groups of skeleton-like people accompanied by SS guards with huge dogs. The prisoners were returning from work. What kind of work did they do that made them so thin? Were they sick? Did they not get food? Everything around me stank with that horrible, thick, chicken-feather smell and looked dark, gray, and lifeless. Threatening. I do not remember any grass, trees, or flowers anywhere.

Finally, we arrived at our barracks in Camp II B, the girls' camp in Birkenau, also referred to as Auschwitz II. The building was a barn originally built for horses. It was filthy. The stink inside was worse than the stench outside. There were no windows on the lower part of the walls for light or ventilation, only across the top above our heads, which made it suffocating. A double row of bricks forming a bench ran down the middle of the barracks. At the end stood a three-hole latrine, another privilege for twins; we did not have to go outside in the big public latrine to go to the bathroom. There were a few hundred twins from ages two to sixteen. We spotted Mrs. Csengeri's daughters there, too, but we did not speak to them at that time.

That first night a pair of Hungarian twins who had been there a while showed us the triple-decker bunks. Miriam and I had a bunk on the bottom.

When the evening meal arrived, all the other children rushed to the doorway. Dinner consisted of a two-and-a-half-inch slice of dark bread and a brownish fluid that everyone called "fake coffee." Miriam and I looked at each other. "We can't eat this," I said to one of the Hungarian twins.

"It's all you will get until tomorrow," she said. "You had better eat it."

"It's not kosher," I said. At home on the farm, we only had kosher food—food that fulfilled the requirements of Jewish dietary law—that Papa blessed before every meal.

The twins laughed at us, but it was not a kind laugh, more like a boy-are-you-stupid laugh. And they greedily wolfed down the bread that Miriam and I offered them.

"We're glad to have the extra bread," they said, "but the two of you are going to have to learn to eat everything if you want to survive. You cannot be fussy, and you cannot worry about whether or not something is kosher."

After the meal, the Hungarian twins and some of the others briefed us. "You are in Birkenau," they told us. "It is part of Auschwitz, but it's three kilometers from the main camp. Auschwitz has one gas chamber and one crematorium."

Miriam said, "I don't understand."

I asked, "What is a gas chamber? What is a crematorium?"

"Follow us, and we'll show you."

The twins led us to the back of the barracks near the door where the barracks supervisor did not notice us. We looked up at the sky. Flames rose from chimneys that towered over Birkenau. Smoke covered the whole camp and fine ash filled the air, making it as dusky as the sky after an explosion of a volcano—it was that thick. Again, we were hit by that terrible smell.

Even though I was afraid to ask, I heard myself saying, "What are they burning so late in the evening?"

"People," said a girl.

"You don't burn people!" I said. "Don't be ridiculous."

"The Nazis do. They want to burn all the Jews."

Somebody else said, "Did you see how the Nazis divided the people arriving on the trains into two groups this morning? They are probably burning one group right now. If the Nazis think you are young and strong enough to work, you are allowed to live. The rest are taken to the gas chambers and gassed to death."

I thought of Mama who was so weak after her long illness.

I thought of Papa, clutching his prayer book.

I thought of our two older sisters.

Deep down, I knew without being told that they had been pushed into the line that had gone to the gas chamber. Against that feeling, I allowed myself to hope that maybe they were still alive. After all, they were older and smarter than Miriam and me.

"We are children," I said. "We can't work, but we're still alive."

"For now," replied a twin. "And it's only because we're twins, and they use us in experiments conducted by Dr. Mengele. He'll be here tomorrow right after roll call."

In a quavering voice, I asked, "What experiments?"

Lea, a twelve-year-old twin, told us to stop worrying and go to bed.

The children slept in their clothes and shoes, so Miriam and I did, too. We lay in our wooden bunk on a straw mattress in our matching dresses. Although I was tired, I could not sleep. Tossing and turning, I noticed something moving on the floor. "There are mice in here!" The scream came out of me without my thinking about it.

"Quiet!" someone said. "Those are not mice, they are rats. They won't hurt you if you don't have any food in your bed. Now go to sleep." I had seen mice before on our farm, but they were not huge like these rats; these rodents were the size of small cats.

I needed to use the latrine and so did Miriam. In the dark, we put our feet down, slowly, carefully, because of the rats. We kicked our shoes back and forth to scare them away. Then we hurried to the end of the barracks. The latrine was about twelve feet square, with dark wooden walls and a cement floor. Latrines are not like bathrooms today; they have floors with holes in them that you have to perch over. They were even worse than the rest of the barracks. Vomit and human feces that had missed the holes of the latrine were everywhere. The smell was hideous.

We stepped inside and I froze. There on the floor in the filth were the dead bodies of three naked children. I had never seen a dead person before. There they lay, on that hard, cold, stinking floor . . . dead. At precisely that moment, I realized that death could happen to Miriam and me. I silently vowed to do everything in my power to make sure that Miriam and I did not end up dead like those children.

We were going to be stronger, smarter, *whatever it took* not to end up that way.

From that point forward, in my mind, we were always going to walk out of the camp alive. I never permitted fears or doubts to dominate my thoughts. As soon as they entered my mind, I pushed them out forcefully. From the moment I left the latrine, I concentrated all my being on one thing: how to survive one more day in this horrible place.

CHAPTER FOUR

In the morning, a whistle shrieked. It was still dark. "Up! Up! Up!" shouted the barracks supervisor, a *Pflegerin*, or nurse, who took care of us. She wore a white coat. "Get ready!" she screeched.

Miriam and I did not know the routine yet. Holding hands we watched the older girls helping little ones prepare for roll call. Outside we lined up in rows of five to be counted. Roll call took half an hour to an hour. Looking back, I do not remember a single child sitting down or crying. Not even the two-year-olds. I think we understood instinctively that our lives depended on cooperation.

After roll call, we went inside to straighten up the barracks. The three dead children Miriam and I had seen at the latrine the night before were no longer on the floor. We learned that when a child died, the other children in the same bunk could not stand lying next to a dead body, so they removed the corpse to the latrine and kept her clothing for themselves.

As for the three dead bodies Miriam and I had seen, adults had put them back into their bunks to be counted. Every day, every child had to be counted, dead or alive. Dr. Mengele knew how many twins he had, and no corpse could be disposed of without following procedure.

That first morning, an SS guard waited at the front of the barracks. "Doctor MENGELE is COMING!" she yelled. The supervisors seemed nervous, twitchy with anticipation of the great man. Miriam and I stood at attention, not daring to move or breathe.

Dr. Josef Mengele entered the barracks. He was dressed elegantly in an SS uniform and tall, shiny black riding boots. He wore white gloves and carried a baton. My first thought was how handsome he was, like a movie star. He strode through the barracks, counting twins at every bunk, with an entourage of eight people accompanying him. We later found out that the group included a Dr. König, a girl who was the interpreter, and several SS guards and assistants. Mengele was never escorted by fewer than eight in his entourage at these barracks checks.

When Dr. Mengele stopped at the bunks containing the three dead bodies, he flew into a rage. "Why did you let these children die?" he screamed at the nurse and SS guards. "I cannot afford to lose even one child!"

Our nurse and the supervisors trembled.

He continued counting until he came to Miriam and me. He stopped and looked at us. I was petrified. Then he moved on. The other children told us that he had been on the selection platform the day before when we had arrived. He was the one who made the selections of the prisoners with a flick of his baton. To the right meant the gas chamber, to the left, the camp and forced labor.

After Mengele left the barracks, we received our morning food rations. Miriam and I drank the fake coffee, although it tasted awful. Most importantly, it was made from boiled water, and we soon learned that meant it was safe and would not give us dysentery—endless diarrhea.

In groups of five, we marched from Birkenau to the labs in Auschwitz. We entered a big two-story brick building. Miriam and I were forced to take off our dresses, underwear, and shoes. There were boys as well as girls: twenty or thirty sets of twins. In the beginning I was shocked at the sight.

I found out later that boy twins stayed in a separate barracks under better conditions than ours. They were cared for by a young Jewish prisoner, formerly an officer in the Czech military, named Zvi Spiegel, whom Mengele had chosen to supervise them. Zvi intervened to help the little boy twins, convincing Mengele to give them better food and to improve their living conditions; Mengele must have figured all this would make them better guinea pigs. So Zvi, also known as the "Twins' Papa," comforted the boys, gave them games to keep their minds active, and taught them bits of geography and math. During the day he would let them kick around a soccer ball made of a bundle of rags to keep them in better physical condition. He also had them memorize each other's names to make them feel human.

We had no such person in our barracks to lead us and help us form friendships. I never went up to another girl and asked her name or told her mine. We were all alone, just twins with numbers, each of us trying to survive. The only person I had to think about was Miriam.

In that brick building, as I looked around, I noticed some fraternal twins but most were identical like Miriam and me. Later, I learned that Dr. Mengele wanted to discover the secret of twinning. One goal of his experiments was to learn how to create blond-haired, blue-eyed babies in multiple numbers to increase the German population. Hitler called Aryans, the blond and blue-eyed, white-skinned Germans "the Master Race"—and we were his human guinea pigs. To study other natural "abnormalities" and to try to figure out how to prevent genetic mutation, the subjects of Mengele's research included dwarfs, people with disabilities, and Romani people (Gypsies). The dwarfs lived in barracks near ours, and we sometimes saw them walking through camp.

All of us sat completely naked on benches. Boys were there, too. It was very cold. We had no place to hide. It was embarrassing to be there without any clothes. Some girls crossed their legs and covered themselves up with their hands. Others shook with fear while SS guards pointed at us and laughed. The nudity was one of the most dehumanizing things in the camp for me.

Dr. Mengele popped in and out to supervise. Other doctors and nurses in white coats who were inmates or prisoners like us observed us and took notes.

First, they measured my head with an instrument called a caliper, made of two pieces of metal, which they pressed against my skull and squeezed. The doctor called out the numbers to an assistant, who wrote notes into a file.

They measured our earlobes; the bridges of our noses; the size of our lips; the width, shape, and color of our eyes. They compared the shade of blue of Miriam's eyes to the blue of my eyes with a chart of eye colors. Over and over, they measured. They spent three to four hours on one ear. Each time the doctors measured me, they measured Miriam to see how we were alike and how we were different. A photographer snapped pictures; an artist drew sketches. Technicians took X-rays, five or six at a time.

Next they asked us questions and gave commands. An inmate who spoke Hungarian and German acted as translator. If I did something, Miriam did the same. "Every time I follow you," Miriam whispered, "they write something down. They want to see which of us is the leader." Of course it was me, just as it had always been. After observing us the previous day in the processing center when I had resisted tattooing, they also knew I was a troublemaker.

We sat there for six to eight hours. I hated every second. Finally, we were allowed to get dressed and were marched back to our barracks for the evening meal: a meager portion of very dark bread, about two-and-one-half inches long.

In the afternoon, our supervising nurse made us learn a song in German. It went, "I am a little German child. If not, phooey!" She put us in a circle and made one girl stand in the center. We had to walk around that girl and sing, "Phooey, phooey, phooey!"

"Dirty, filthy Jews!" the nurse shouted at us. "Swine!" She loved that song. It meant we children were disgusting. We hated that nurse. We called her "Snake" behind her back. She had thick legs and long black hair that she wore in a braid. Snake kept taunting us. "Who do you think you are?" she asked.

We did not answer. She did not expect an answer, either. "You think you are so smart because you are still alive?" asked Snake. "You're going to be dead before long. We're going to kill all of you."

For the first day or two, Miriam and I cried and cried. But we soon realized that crying would not help anything. We mostly felt numb.

Staying alive was the most important thing. We knew we were alive because of the experiments. Because of a fortunate accident of nature.

Because we were Mengele's twins.

CHAPTER FIVE

Being in Auschwitz was like being in a car accident every single day. Every single day something terrifying happened.

Within two weeks, Miriam and I had to have our heads shaved. Like all the twins in our barracks, we were infested with head lice. Head lice, I learned, lay their eggs on human hair. And they can go from one head to another. The only way to get rid of them is to use a special shampoo, or chemical treatment, and comb hair daily with a fine-toothed nit comb. We had none of these things, so lice multiplied and spread from person to person, onto clothing and bedding— they were everywhere. Lice and fleas nested in our blankets, straw mattresses, and dresses. We were constantly scratching ourselves. Even with our hair chopped off, we still had lice! Miriam and I constantly picked lice off each other and tried to squeeze them dead between our fingernails.

Once a week, twins had the privilege of taking a shower. Each of us received a bar of soap. In the huge shower room, we took off our clothes and left them in a pile to be disinfected. Later, I learned that the chemical used to disinfect our clothing, Zyklon B, was one of the three chemicals used to gas people to death at Auschwitz. The Nazis combined Zyklon B, which came in gray-blue pellets, with hydrogen cyanide and diatomite to form the chemical mix for mass murder in the gas chambers. The gas, mixed with burning flesh and bones, created that stench I had noticed the first day. It is not a smell a human can ever forget.

Miriam and I stayed close. We always stayed close. Before we washed, we stood in a tub of whitish liquid. It burned my legs and left red blotches. Sometimes the supervisors wiped down our heads and bodies, and the disinfectant stung my eyes. Forty or fifty twins showered at the same time. Dr. Mengele wanted us to be clean and did occasionally have his assistants make

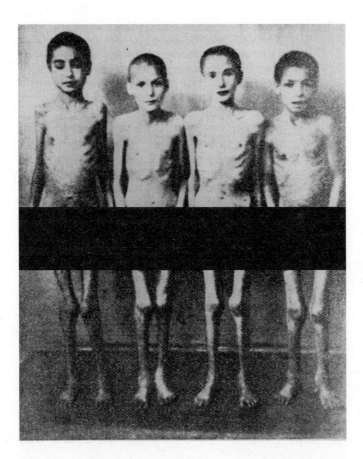

Twins in one of the Auschwitz laboratories

Josef Mengele

attempts to clean up our barracks. Yet the filth and lice from the camp would always return, and we coped with it as best we could.

One time we saw some boys at the shower. I remember looking at them and thinking, "They're so skinny. I'm glad I don't look like that." Actually, I probably *did* look like that. Miriam, too. Her eyes were sunken, and I could count every bone in her body. But I did not feel skinny and pathetic. I needed to see myself as strong.

Dr. Mengele set up a routine for us to follow. Three days a week we were forced to march to the labs in Auschwitz for intensive studies that left us exhausted. The other three days we were in the blood labs in Birkenau. One day melded into the next. Every morning after roll call, Mengele came to our barracks for inspection. Smiling, he called us *meine Kinder,* my children. Some of the twins liked him and called him Uncle Mengele. Not I. I was terrified of him. Even in those days, I knew he did not care about us like a real doctor.

On Tuesdays, Thursdays, and Saturdays, we went to the blood lab. Miriam and I sat on a bench with another set of twin sisters. Someone tied our upper left arms and right arms with thin, flexible, rubber hoses. Two people worked on me at the same time. A doctor jabbed a needle into my left arm to take blood. He withdrew a vial's worth and then stuck me again. I could see hands taking away bright red vials of my blood. I remembered wondering, "How much blood can I lose and still live?" Meanwhile a different doctor gave me an injection of something in my right arm. He stuck five needles in without removing the first one. What was he shooting into my remaining blood?

I hated these injections. But I refused to cry out in pain because I did not want to let the Nazis know they were hurting me. I coped by turning my head away and counting the shots until it was over.

On our way back to our barracks, Miriam and I did not talk about the injections. I took those injections as the price we had to pay to survive: We gave them our blood, our bodies, our pride, our dignity, and in turn

Lagerarzt des . 10.AUG.1944 Birkenau, 8. August 1944
KL Auschwitz II.
(Frauenlager)

An das
Hygiene-Institut der Waffen-SS u.Polizei,
A u s c h w i t z.

Anbei wird Blutmaterial zur Untersuchung auf
Rest N, Na Cl., Takata-Ara, Vitamin C eingesandt:

1. H.Nr.A 5131 Malek Judith
2. "   80912   Kohnstein Emilie.
3. " A 7736   Malek Salomon.
4. " A 5771   Molnar Maria
5. " A 6035   Moskowicz Helena
6. " A 3626   Weiss Olga
7. " A 7063   Mozes Eva
8. " A 7259   Neuschloss Judith
9. "   80913   Kohstein Gisela.

Der Lagerarztdes
KL Auschwitz-II.
SS-Untersturmführer

Original document showing that Eva's blood samples were
tested for urea nitrogen, sodium chloride, globulin, and
vitamin C. There are also documents showing tests for
syphilis and scarlet fever.

To Whom It May Concern:

I, Werner L. Loewenstein, M.D., a physician educated in Germany, resident of Terre Haute, IN, located in Vigo County, have translated a document from The Camp Physician of The Concentration Camp Auschwitz II.

The Camp Physician   Birkenau, August 2, 1944
Concentration Camp Auschwitz II
(Women Camp)

To The Hygienic Institute of The Army SS and Police,

<u>A u s c h w i t z</u>

Enclosed are blood samples for examination of Urea Nitrogen, Sodium Chloride, Takata-Ara, and Vitamin C.

A list of nine names follows—see attached document.

Signed by The Camp Physician
Concentration Camp Auschwitz II
Mengele (looks like Mengele's signature)
SS Sub Storm Leader

I certify that I have translated the above from the attached document, and that this is an accurate and true representation of what is contained therein.

Werner L. Loewenstein

Werner L. Loewenstein

State of Indiana
County of Vigo

Before me, the undersigned, a Notary Public in and for said County and State, this 13th day of __April__ 1985 Werner L. Loewenstein personally appeared and acknowledged the execution of the above translation.

Witness my hand and Notarial Seal

Signature

Resident of Vigo County

My Commission Expires
July 13, 1988

English translation of the document on the previous page

they let us live one more day. I cannot remember a single twin who did not cooperate.

In those days we didn't know what the experiments were for or what we were injected with. Later, we found out that Dr. Mengele purposely gave some twins dangerous, life-threatening diseases such as scarlet fever, then followed them with injections of something else to see if it cured the disease. Some injections were attempts to change the color of eyes. Older girls, many years after we were all liberated, told us Mengele had taken them to a lab and given them a transfusion of blood from a boy, and had transfused their blood into the bodies of boys. He wanted to discover a way to change girls into boys and boys into girls. Many of these details I learned forty years later, such as the twin teenage boys who had some of their private parts cut off in Mengele's quest to see if he could turn them into girls. One of those boys died in his bed right next to his twin, who said later, "I could feel my brother's body turning cold."

It was said at the time that six sets of twins had gone to that lab and been killed. I never witnessed anyone being killed; I only knew that some of the twins disappeared. But I did eventually learn that the rumors were correct, that twins were dying from some of the experiments. We were told they had become "very sick." Then Mengele would simply replace them with fresh sets of twins who had just arrived on transport trains. That is how even the most privileged prisoners at Auschwitz were viewed. Not even Mengele's favorites were treated as humans. We were replaceable. Disposable.

What was not replaced were our pretty, matching dresses, which got so worn out we could no longer wear them. We were given women's clothing. But the clothing was too big, so Miriam and I tied strings around our waists to hold up the dresses. In the tops of our dresses we tucked anything we were carrying, like a metal cup or a piece of bread saved from the night before.

In the morning before roll call and on the days we went to the blood lab, we helped take care of the younger children. Outside our barracks, we had a fenced-in yard where we played with them. The older girls taught Miriam and me how to knit. We pulled pieces of barbed wire from the fencing, hit the wires against stone to loosen the barbs, and pulled them off. It took a long time. Then we sharpened the points of the wire on some rocks to make knitting needles. One of the twins had an old sweater that we took apart, saving the yarn. Each girl took a turn knitting until the yarn from the sweater was all used up. Then the next person would unravel the yarn, and we would start all over again. It was not about a finished product—a cap, a scarf, or socks. Knitting took our minds off of our troubles.

But death and danger were never far away. One day when we were outside, a cart of dead bodies rolled by. We ran to the fence to see if we recognized any of the corpses.

One girl cried out, "Mama! It's my mama!" and burst into tears. She sobbed, her anguish crescendoing into wails, as the cart continued on its way. I felt sorry for her, but I did not know what to say.

At that moment, I realized that maybe our mother had also gone by on a cart of bodies; we just hadn't seen her. Every day those carts went by. Sometimes the prisoners on them were dead, sometimes only mostly dead; regardless, they were all being carted away to their final resting place. Until that moment, I had stopped thinking about my family. Maybe it was due to the bread we ate each evening that supposedly contained not only sawdust but a powder called bromide that made us forget memories of home, a sedative of some kind. Whatever it was or was not, I could not feel sorry for myself, for Miriam, for anyone. I could not think of myself as a victim, or I knew I would perish. It was simple. For me, there was no room for any thought except survival. At night, Miriam and I lay in our bunk with two other sets of twins. We snuggled close but did not talk or whisper. If I had told Miriam how hungry and miserable I was, it would have only made things worse. In the darkness, I heard a whistle, a car, or motorcycle going by. Noises of marching, moaning, vomiting, barking, and crying punctuated the hush of camp—an orchestra accompanying the pervasive human misery.

Occasionally, when our supervisors were asleep, our old friend from the neighboring village, Mrs. Csengeri, sneaked into our barracks to see her twin daughters. She was a smart, quick-witted woman. Upon her arrival at Auschwitz, she had convinced Dr. Mengele that she could help him by giving him information about her twins, so she had been allowed to stay in the women's barracks. Mrs. Csengeri brought her children food, underwear, hats, things she had taken or "organized." "Organizing" was camp language for stealing from the Nazis. I envied those girls for having a mother who was still alive and caring for them; Miriam and I had only each other.

I could not think about Mama, Papa, or our older sisters anymore. I had to worry about Miriam and myself. I had to repeat to myself over and over:

Just one more day.

Just one more experiment.

Just one more injection.

Just please, please, don't let us get sick.

CHAPTER SIX

One Saturday in July, we marched to the lab, where I was injected with something that must have been a germ. They gave the injection only to me, not my twin. Years later, Miriam and I guessed that they chose me because they had observed that I was stronger.

What I was not prepared for was that this injection would make me sick. During the night ,I ran a high fever. My head pounded. My skin burned dry. My body shook so hard that I could not sleep, despite my fatigue. I woke Miriam.

"I'm v-very s-s-sick," I whispered through chattering teeth into her ear.

She was instantly awake, instantly worried. "What shall we do?"

"I d-d-d-don't know," I said. "L-l-let's t-t-try to hide

it and pre-pre-pretend that I'm all r-r-r-ight."

By Monday morning when we stood outside for roll call, I was really dizzy. My arms and legs were covered with red patches and swollen to twice their size. They were so painful, I thought I would explode out of my skin. I shivered with chills. The sunshine warmed me up a little, and I tried desperately not to tremble so that the *Pflegerinnen*, or nurses, would not notice I was sick. I did not want to be taken to the infirmary. On two occasions, a twin in our barracks had become sick and had been taken to the infirmary. They never came back. The matching twin had then also been taken away and they did not return either. We assumed both twins were killed once one of them got sick. I could not let this happen to Miriam and me. Why should she die just because I might die?

Just before roll call actually began, the air-raid sirens sounded a loud, piercing warning: We were going to be bombed. With shivering delight I watched the SS guards run for cover as a plane with an American flag painted on one of the wings circled the concentration camp. I thought to myself, "Look at these Nazis, the bullies of the world, running like scaredy cats!" I recognized the Stars and Stripes because our aunt, Papa's sister, lived in Cleveland, Ohio, and before the war she had sent letters to us with stamps printed with the American flag. Now the plane flew low and made a yellow smoke circle above the entire camp. Even in those days, we knew that the plane would not bomb inside the circle. More planes followed, and in the distance we heard bombs exploding. The American planes gave us hope. The planes meant that help was coming. Someday soon we would be freed and get to go home—if we could just stay alive long enough. We kids clapped; those were our moments of glory.

But on our next visit to the lab, the doctors did not bother to examine me. They called my number and took my temperature. I knew I was in trouble. Immediately, two *Pflegerinnen* put me in some kind of car or jeep and drove me away. I did not even get to see Miriam before I was taken away. It was the first time in the camp that we had been separated. Staying together, counting on each other, having another human being to really care about had kept us both from feeling so alone.

The nurses took me to the infirmary: Building #21, a filthy barracks close to the gas chamber and flaming chimneys. A putrid stench filled the air. Bunks three tiers high held people who were half dead. Row after row, they formed a sea of human beings dying a slow death. All of them were grown-ups. As I walked past, they reached out their bony fingers:

"Please!"

"Water! Water!"

"Food! Please! Anything?"

"Help me!"

They all seemed to be crying, unable to move. It looked like there were more hands reaching out than there could have been people. I can recall reading about a Valley of Death in the Bible; the infirmary felt like that valley. It was the worst place I had ever been.

I was put into a room with two older girls, Vera and Tamara. Each of the girls was the sister of another pair of twins. They had chicken pox, so they were not too sick. Our room was small, but only we three shared it—another privilege for twins.

That night the time for dinner came and went. We received no food ration.

"Why aren't they feeding us?" I asked. "We should be getting bread."

Vera said, "No one here gets anything to eat because people are brought here to die or are taken from here to die in the gas chamber."

"They don't want to waste food on the dying," said Tamara.

I cannot die, I told myself. I will not die.

That night I was too sick to feel hungry. I found it hard to sleep without Miriam beside me, cuddling. In the dark I heard people moaning and screaming in pain. Their screams cut into me. I had never heard so many voices wailing, howling, and bellowing.

The next day a truck came. The sickest people were thrown onto the truck bed to be taken directly to the gas chamber. They shrieked and struggled as some of them were tossed on top of people who were already dead.

"Am I going to the gas chamber?" I thought. The gas chamber was always there, next to the crematorium belching its stink of burning human hair, bones, and flesh into the air all around us. The gas chamber was a real possibility for any of us in that camp—but more so for those of us in the infirmary. Twice a week those trucks would come. Years later, I learned that right before the bodies were thrown into the crematorium, a group of workers would pull out gold teeth and remove any jewelry. The Nazis collected an average of seventy-six pounds of gold from the bodies every single day. Someone was getting rich.

The morning after I arrived, Mengele and a team of four other doctors came to see me. They discussed my case as though they were in a regular hospital. Although they spoke in German, I understood a lot of what they were saying. Dr. Mengele laughed and said about me with a smirk, "Too bad. She is so young and has only two weeks to live."

"How could he know that?" I wondered. They had not run any more tests on me after the poisonous injection. I've since learned that Mengele knew what disease they had infected me with and how it would progress. It might have been beriberi or spotted fever. In all the years since, I have never found out for sure.

As I lay in the bed and listened to Mengele and the other doctors, I tried not to let on that I grasped the meaning of their words. I said to myself, "I am not dead. I refuse to die. I am going to outsmart those doctors, prove Dr. Mengele wrong, and get out of here alive." Above all, I knew I had to get back to Miriam.

During those first few days, I was running a very high fever, but no one gave me food, medicine, or water. They only checked my temperature. I was so thirsty, desperate for water, my mouth so dry I thought I could not breathe much longer.

There was a faucet at the far end of the barracks. I remember sliding out of bed, opening the door, and crawling on the floor to reach that faucet. The rough cement scraped my skin, chilling my belly. I stretched my hands forward and dragged my body on all fours, creeping slowly along that floor coated with muck and slime. Sometimes I passed out, then woke up and inched onward.

I am going to get well, I kept repeating to myself.

I must live. I must survive.

The need to get water overpowered me. The strangest thing is that I do not remember drinking the water. I must have, because there was no other way I could have survived. I do not even recall how I got back to my bunk in the room I shared with the other girls. Yet every night for two weeks I pulled myself to that faucet.

After my first week in the infirmary, Miriam found out that I was not receiving any food. Mrs. Csengeri, our old friend, told her. Mrs. Csengeri acted as a messenger, sneaking from barracks to barracks as she visited her own twin daughters. Miriam started saving her bread for me and gave it to Mrs. Csengeri to deliver into my hands. Imagine Miriam's willpower, a ten-year-old deciding not to eat for a week! That daily piece of bread from my twin sister helped save my life and made me more determined to be reunited with her. After two weeks, like a miracle, my fever broke! I started feeling stronger.

One night, I woke up and saw the silhouette of our block supervisor: slim, dark. Every once in a while, she stole into our room at night and gave us food. "Here is a piece of bread for you," she said quietly, putting it on my bed. "If anybody finds out, I'll be punished." Once, she even gave Vera, Tamara, and me a piece of her birthday cake. What a treat! It was so good, so sweet. We devoured it, licking our fingers and then licking the paper that had held the cake. Even in Auschwitz, some people were humane.

However, when I think back on those days, I am not sure why she did not give me water when I was so sick the first two weeks. I can only guess that she saved her efforts for those who looked as though they would survive.

As I gained strength I wanted to get out of that infirmary as fast as I could, but I was still running a fever. Dr. Mengele and his team came twice a day to check my fever chart. I had to convince them that my temperature was going down so that I could be sent back to the twins' barracks. So I thought of a plan.

Vera and Tamara taught me how to read the thermometer. When the nurse, a fellow prisoner, came in and placed the thermometer under my arm she told me to keep it there until she returned. After she left the room, I took the thermometer out, read it, and shook it down a little. Then I put it back in my armpit almost all the way, letting it stick out the back so that it would not register any change. The nurse returned, read my temperature, and wrote it down. I had to be very careful to do this gradually so that Mengele would not get suspicious about my recovery. The plan worked! Three weeks later I was released.

Joyfully, I returned to my sister. Now that we were together, I knew I would get well. But I was shocked by Miriam's appearance. She had an empty look in her eyes and sat staring into space. She looked weak and lifeless.

"What's wrong?" I asked her. "What's happened? What have they done to you?"

"Nothing," said Miriam. "Leave me alone, Eva. I can't talk about it."

I knew that our separation had affected Miriam

badly. She had thought I was not coming back; the thought of being all alone had made her lose hope. In camp language she had become a *Muselmann*, a zombie, someone who no longer had the spirit to fight for life.

For the first two weeks while I was gone, she did not go to the lab. She was kept in solitary confinement, guarded by SS at all times. At first, Miriam did not know what was happening to me, but my twin must have sensed they were waiting for something. When I did not die as Mengele expected, Miriam was taken to the labs and given many injections that made her sick. The shots would stunt the growth of her kidneys, keeping them the size of a ten-year-old's. I never discovered the purpose of this experiment on my sister.

However, I did learn that Mengele had planned for me to die from the disease I had been given. Dr. Miklós Nyiszli, a Jewish prisoner and pathologist, wrote and published an eyewitness account about how Mengele routinely ordered pathologists to perform autopsies on twins who had died within hours of each other, a unique opportunity to compare the effects of disease on healthy and diseased bodies that were identical in most other ways. If I had died in the infirmary, Miriam would have been rushed to the lab and killed with a shot of chloroform to her heart. Simultaneous autopsies would have compared my diseased organs to her healthy ones. If the organs held any scientific interest, Mengele would have examined them himself and sent them on to the Anthropological Institute at Berlin-Dahlem in a package marked "War Material—Urgent."

However, I, a ten-year-old girl, had triumphed over Mengele by surviving his experiment. Now it was up to me to help my twin sister get better. I could not lose her. It was that simple. How to accomplish it was another thing.

CHAPTER SEVEN

At Auschwitz-Birkenau we never knew what tomorrow would bring. Each day brought challenges for us to survive. Miriam was very sick with something besides just the incessant diarrhea of dysentery. Although everyone including me had dysentery, Miriam had given up the will to live. I had to find some way to help her to get better. Part of the reason she was so sick was the injections she had been given while I was away.

The word around camp was that potatoes would strengthen us and heal dysentery. In Auschwitz, people "organized" anything needed for survival from the Nazis. Inmates viewed organizing as a victorious action. The problem was that I had never stolen anything before in my life except for one thing: a cup.

Once, on our way to the shower, as we marched in a

row of five, we had approached a pile of pots and pans. I had edged from my place in the middle of the row to the outside. I leaped up, seized a cup, tucked it into the loose top of my dress, and marched on as though nothing had happened. If the SS guard accompanying us saw me, he said nothing.

Rumor was that anyone caught stealing would be hanged, just like those who tried to escape. The Nazis had made us watch these hangings before, telling us to observe closely, that this was what would happen to us if we stole or tried to get away. I remember thinking to myself, "Yes, life is so wonderful here. Why on earth would we try to escape?" I resolved to find a way to take some potatoes to help Miriam get well. I did not know what would happen to me if I dared to take potatoes, but I knew it could be death. A gibbet, the wooden frame for hanging people, stood in front of Block 11. Even if that is what awaited me if I were caught, for Miriam, the risk was imperative. I could not let Miriam die.

Other twins in our barracks were cooking potatoes at night, so I asked them where I could get some potatoes. They told me the only place to get potatoes was the kitchen, so I volunteered to be a food carrier. This meant I would be one of two children hauling soup in a huge container the size of a thirty-gallon garbage can from the kitchen at the end of the camp to our barracks. It took twenty minutes to walk there; lugging back the heavy filled can took us even longer. The first time I volunteered, I was not chosen. The next day, I volunteered again and was picked along with another twin to get the daily soup, a watery liquid that occasionally had a bit of potato.

As soon as I entered the kitchen, I spotted a long metal table that held pots and pans. Beneath, I noticed two sacks of potatoes. For a moment, I hesitated. If I were caught, I could die, but if I did not try, Miriam would die.

I bent down and peered around to see if anybody was watching me. My heart pounding so hard I felt it in my ear canals, I reached into the sack and snatched two potatoes. Somebody grabbed me by my head and pulled me up. It was the kitchen worker, a fat woman prisoner wearing a striped scarf on her head.

"You cannot do that!" she yelled in my face.

"Do what, Madame?" My eyes were wide with false innocence.

"It's not nice to steal. Put those back."

I dropped the potatoes back into the sack. I expected to be dragged to the gallows immediately, but that did not happen. I almost burst out laughing with relief when I realized that my only punishment would be that scolding. I had just learned that being a Mengele twin meant that no one dared deliberately harm us as long as Mengele wanted us alive. He needed us to continue his experiments.

But I still had a worry that the kitchen worker would report my attempted crime to the *blokova*, our block supervisor, and I would not be allowed to carry food again. The next day, however, I volunteered and was chosen again.

This time it was easier to organize potatoes without getting caught. I was not nearly as nervous, because I knew the worst that could happen to me was a tongue-lashing. Once I reached the sacks, I quickly grasped three potatoes from under the table and hid them in my dress. This time, no one saw. Success! That tiny cache of potatoes was one of the greatest treasures I had ever had. I could hardly *wait* for evening.

Any secret activities like cooking had to be done at night after the *blokova* and assistant supervisor had gone to bed in their little rooms at the front of the barracks. One of the twins had brought a few pieces of charcoal that she had organized during the day. We had an oven at the end of the brick bench that ran down the center of the barracks, and we made a small fire in it. Someone stood guard at the *blokova*'s closed door in case she woke up. Other girls stayed at the entrance of the barracks and signaled by tapping their feet if anyone was approaching. In the dark, we took turns cooking.

I used my own pot and boiled my potatoes—peels, spots, dirt, and all! Then Miriam and I had our feast. We ate the potatoes without salt or butter, but they tasted delicious to us. They filled us with warmth and raised our spirits. I would have given Miriam all of the food, but I was starving and needed strength to take care of us both.

Every day after that, I volunteered to carry the vat of soup, though I was only chosen maybe one or two times each week. But with each turn I became better at organizing. I always took more potatoes than we needed for that day. As a result, Miriam and I usually had potatoes three times a week.

Sometimes, Mrs. Csengeri sneaked in at night and cooked the potatoes she had organized for her twin daughters. As soon as one person finished cooking, another took her place at the oven. We formed a little brigade and always had people posted on guard duty to make sure we did not get caught.

Everyone knew the system and the rules. Despite the fact that everyone was skin and bones, hunger reminding us we were still alive, we did not try to take one another's food.

The potatoes I brought Miriam worked like medicine. She became healthier, stronger, and willing to fight for her own life. I can say, and it would not have hurt her feelings, that my sister would have died then if it had not been for me. And. in turn, taking care of Miriam had helped me become sturdier and more forceful, too. Because we were twins, we clung to each other. Because we were sisters, we depended on each other. Because we were family, we did not let go.

At Auschwitz, dying was so easy. Surviving was a full- time job.

CHAPTER EIGHT

As the summer of 1944 turned to autumn, things were changing. More and more airplanes roared overhead and bombed Nazi headquarters and factories. Sometimes there were two or three air raids a day. Although we had no radio or news, we realized the good guys were coming to free us. I had to keep my twin sister and myself alive until they arrived. Her life was my mission and responsibility. But conditions in the camp were not getting any better. In some ways, they were worse.

During the night of October 7th, the sound of a huge explosion woke us up. Sirens wailed. Dogs barked. What was happening? Later we found out that Jews of the *Sonderkommando* (prisoners forced to burn corpses of fellow prisoners) had rebelled and blown up Crematorium IV in Birkenau. They had used explosives smuggled to them by a group of Jewish girls working in the Nazi explosives factory. The men of the *Sonderkommando* had decided they would rather go down fighting than die in the gas chamber. They wanted to take revenge for the deaths of families and friends.

Rumors circulated that as the Allied Forces—the American, British, and Soviet armies—approached, the SS would kill everyone in the camp. Nevertheless, Dr. Mengele continued his experiments, still hoping to make an important scientific discovery.

At that time, we did not know that orders had come from the Nazi high command for Dr. Mengele to "liquidate" the Gypsy camp consisting of more than two thousand Romani prisoners, mostly women and children. Although Mengele had tried to preserve the Gypsies for his research, he followed orders. They were taken to the gas chambers to be killed and then incinerated.

Miriam and I and all the twins in our barracks were marched from our camp to the Gypsy camp, now empty. The inmates had left behind blankets and colorful paintings on the walls. We did not know why the Nazis had transferred us to their camp. It was close to a gas chamber and crematorium, and the word went around that we were next to be gassed.

On that first day, we stood outside in the cold for roll call, patches of snow covering the ground, from 5am until 4pm. It was the longest roll call we had ever been through because a prisoner was missing. The smells of the crematorium were thick in the air, mixing with cold and fog. My feet froze and so did my sister's. We never found out to where the prisoner had escaped.

For the next few weeks, we stayed in the Gypsy camp, living in the shadow of the crematorium with constant dread that we would be killed. We never knew why that did not happen. Maybe we were saved by orders from Berlin to stop gassing the Jews. The Nazis by then must have known they were losing the war. Maybe they wanted to hide the evidence of their atrocities.

Then, in early January 1945, the SS began to order people out of the barracks to go on forced marches. *"Raus! Raus!* Out! Out!" they shouted. "Everybody out! We are taking you away for your own protection." We heard that thousands of people were now being marched deep into Germany.

"I am not going to leave the barracks," I said to Miriam. "I am not going on any march." I figured that the Nazis had not been particularly nice to us when they were winning the war, so they certainly would not be any nicer when they were losing it. We stayed.

To my surprise, no one came to get us. The Nazis were in such a hurry to get everybody out that they did not bother checking each barracks. Some of the twins remained with us, including Mrs. Csengeri and her daughters. At the time, I did not know that many people had also chosen to stay behind.

The next morning, we woke up and realized we had missed roll call. We discovered that the Nazis were gone . . . or so it seemed. We saw no guards, no SS, no Dr. Mengele.

The joy and happiness we felt! The Nazis were gone! Now we were on our own. I spent my time trying to find food, water, and blankets to keep my sister and me alive.

One of the men prisoners had cut an opening in

the barbed wire so that we could walk from one camp to another. Two girls and I went to search for things, roaming from area to area. I badly needed shoes. I was still wearing the ones from home that I had on when I had arrived at Auschwitz. The soles kept flapping open. I tied them with string, but it was still rather hard to walk. Miriam's shoes were in better condition because she had stayed in the barracks to guard our few belongings whenever I went out organizing.

The girls and I went to the place where the Nazis had kept all the clothes, shoes, and blankets they had taken from the prisoners. It was a huge building the Nazis called "Canada," perhaps because they saw the country of Canada as a place of abundance. Piles of belongings rose to the ceiling. I rummaged through shoe after shoe after shoe, but I could not find any that fit, so I finally chose a pair that was two sizes too big. I filled the toe areas with some rags and tied them with string. At least my feet were now warm. I grabbed some coats and blankets for us and brought them back to the barracks where we bundled up.

One afternoon, I went to the kitchen to organize food. A couple of kids and some grown-ups who had stayed behind were already there taking bread.

Holding four or five bread loaves in my arms, I heard the strange sound of a car. "The Nazis are gone, so whose car is coming?" I wondered. We ran outside to see. There was a jeep-like car, and four Nazis holding machine guns jumped out and began spraying bullets in every direction.

I remember seeing a barrel of a gun pointed at my head, three to four feet from me, then I faded away.

When I woke up, I thought I was dead. All around me I saw bodies.

OK. So we are all dead, I thought. Then I moved my arms. Then I moved my legs. I touched the person beside me, but there was no movement. Her body was cold. Aha! *She* was dead, but I was alive!

I stood up, thankful to be alive. I thought it must have been a guardian angel that made me faint before the bullets hit me, because I did not have any time to think or do anything to save myself.

I raced back to the barracks. "Miriam?" I called as I burst inside.

There she was. "What happened?" she asked, eyes round with fear.

"The Nazis are back!" I said and added, "I wonder why they are back? They almost killed me!" I told her what had happened and how terrified I had been. "We don't have any bread. I was so frightened, I just ran for my life."

"Oh, Eva," she said, "what if you had been killed?"

We did not talk about that "what if" anymore. We just hugged and hugged.

That same night we were awakened by smoke and heat. Flames shot down from the roof. We could feel searing heat from the flames through the barracks walls. The barracks were on fire! We grabbed our stuff and ran outside. The Nazis were back at the camp, no longer in hiding, probably trying to destroy the evidence of their crimes.

Flames reddened the sky as far as we could see. SS guards had blown up a crematorium and the building called Canada. Shirts and dresses from Canada flew through the air amidst the sparks and ashes. The Allies were attacking and bombs lit the sky. It looked like the whole world was on fire.

Thousands of people surged out of the rows and rows of barracks. The same SS guards I had seen at the kitchen lined us up for marching. "Anyone who doesn't march quickly will be shot!" screamed a guard. He shot randomly into the crowd as a warning.

"Miriam, stay with me," I whispered. We did not know where we were going. I held on to her hand very tightly. We worked our way into the middle of the group. It was safer than being in the front or the back where we might attract attention. If they started shooting, we would be surrounded by other people.

The crowd swept us along. Being pushed and jostled in that big crowd, it was a struggle to stay in the middle. The SS kept shooting randomly as they herded us. As bodies fell to the ground around us, our fear increased. All of the children and the older people who had not been taken in the earlier marches were in this march.

Later, we learned that 8,200 people, including us, marched from Birkenau that night. In one hour, 1,200 were killed on the way. Only 7,000 people arrived at the barracks.

Forced by the wave of the crowd, we finally arrived back at the barracks in Auschwitz. It was still the middle of the night, but the brick buildings glowed in the klieg lights. Not knowing what would happen next, people started pushing hard, shoving to get inside the two-story building. Miriam and I also raced toward those barracks for shelter.

The SS guards inexplicably disappeared.

And somehow, I cannot remember how it happened, somehow in the shuffle I lost my twin sister.

"Miriam?" I called. "Miriam! Miriam! Where are you?"

I whirled around and around. She was not there, not anywhere!

As I began to panic, my heart clobbered in my chest, my breath rushed out of me in short bursts, my face burned hot despite the cold. My eyes, darting this way and that, filled with fearful tears.

"What if Miriam winds up in another barracks?" I thought.

"What if she gets transported somewhere?

"What if she gets hurt?

"What if she dies? Who would know to tell me?

"What if I never see her again!"

I left the two-story building and half walked, half ran from barracks to barracks, calling her name. "Miriam! MIR- IAM! MI-RI-AM!"

I asked anyone and everyone whether they had seen a girl who looked just like me. "Her name is Miriam," I told them, "Miriam Mozes. Please, please. Have you seen a girl named Miriam?"

Some kind people must have seen my desperation, my panic. They helped me by joining in, yelling her name: "Miriam Mozes! Miriam Mozes!" But no matter where I went, no matter where I looked, no matter how loudly I yelled, I could not find her.

After a while, when Miriam did not answer, the people stopped helping me search. "Keep searching," they urged me, pity in their eyes, their own exhaustion making their bodies limp. "She has to be here somewhere."

"Miriam! Miriam!" I did not let thirty seconds go by without yelling her name.

While I saw pity and concern in some people's eyes, other people did not care, could not be bothered. So many of them had had enough and did not have even an ounce of concern left for anyone else. "So you're looking for your sister? Big deal! I don't have anybody."

I wanted to yell at them that Miriam was more than a sister. She was my other self. Our survival depended on each other! I could not stop to think about these hopeless souls. I had to find her. I had to.

I kept searching. "Miriam! Miriam!" I cried, my voice growing more hoarse, fainter. I was hungry and tired. But I did not allow myself to sit down to rest. I did not stop. Terrified, I went from one building to another, unable to give up my search. So many emaciated people, their thin prison garb clothing their pitiful bodies, were blocking my vision everywhere I looked. There seemed to be so many other people! They all looked the same to me because they were not Miriam. What could have happened to her? In one quick moment, dashing for safety, we had been separated! What had we done? I kept on.

My legs shuffling forward, my arms pumping to keep me moving, I did not let myself think of hunger, of the pains in my gut, of the dryness making my tongue stick to the roof of my mouth. None of it mattered. "Miriam! Miriam Mozes! Miriam!"

Hours and hours, minutes and minutes, seconds and seconds—all piled on top of another in my panic. I had been searching for twenty-four hours. No Miriam! She could not have simply disappeared. I refused to accept that. Where was she?

I was stumbling about in a near-stupor of desperation and exhaustion when I went through yet another doorway.

"Miriam! Miriam Mozes! Miri—"

I bumped into someone about my height. "Sorry!" I was about to lurch past the person when it hit me: It was Miriam. "Miriam! MIRIAM!" I fell into her arms. She fell into mine. "Where were you? I've been looking, looking, looking! What happened?"

"I have been searching for *you*!" she insisted. "What happened to you?"

We hugged, we kissed. Gripping one another, we both slid to the floor to rest, crying and hanging on to each other. "Eva, where were you?" she asked me through her tears. "We made such a mistake by racing. I thought I would never see you again."

"No. I could not think too much about that. I had to find you!" I insisted. Then I admitted the truth to her. "I was desperate."

I sank into her arms, feeling like it was Hanukkah. It was a miracle!

I had the strongest feeling of relief and love that I have ever felt in my whole life. I pulled away to look at her scrawny face and then put my arms around her again, holding her tight. Those twenty-four hours of searching for her had felt like forever. The more I held on to her, the more I felt sure we would never be parted again. "I am so glad I found you," I told her, filled with more emotion than I could express.

Miriam reached out her hand. "Look!" she said. There she held a piece of chocolate. "Someone gave me this when I was searching for you."

My eyes opened wide. She offered it to me.

I broke it in half, and we savored it in this sweetest of moments.

"From now on, always hold my hand," I said. "Never let go."

Miriam agreed. "Yes, we must never be separated again."

"This is our lucky barracks!" I said.

"Then let's take a little nap here," Miriam said, sinking lower against the wall. "I'm so tired."

Our hands tightly entwined, our bodies close for comfort, we shut our weary eyes. No matter what happened next, we knew we had each other.

CHAPTER NINE

For the next nine days, Miriam and I were on our own, looking out for ourselves like everyone else was doing. We stayed in our lucky barracks with other sets of twins and adult women. My daily task was to find food for Miriam and me. Miriam's feet were frostbitten from that long roll call at the Gypsy camp, so she protected our blankets and bowls while I went organizing with two other girls.

The girls and I broke into Nazi storage places and buildings where the SS had lived. Twice we went into Nazi headquarters, a nice house with nice furniture. Before that, I had not known such a place existed. Luxurious living right in the middle of a Nazi death camp.

We saw food on the table that looked awfully good.

It looked freshly prepared, delectable! In fact, it looked too good. I wondered why the Nazis would leave such good food behind. Was something wrong with it? Out of hunger I snatched some up. But just before eating it, I stopped and put it back. Later, I talked to people in the camp who said that the Nazis had purposely left poisoned food so that prisoners like me would eat it and die.

Another time, the girls and I found huge containers of sauerkraut. We ate the food, and since we had no water to drink and there was no snow on the ground to melt, we drank the sauerkraut juice. In the kitchen, we grabbed bread. For us it was a feast.

By this time we were skillful at scrounging for something to eat. I had organized a scarf, and it became our most valuable tool. In a basement, we came upon a huge pile of flour. I straightened out my square scarf and filled it with flour. Back in the barracks we mixed the flour with some liquid and baked a cake on top of the stove. It was like the unleavened bread the Jews had eaten when, in the Bible, they had had to leave Egypt in a hurry, with no time to allow the bread to rise. It was concentration camp Passover *matzoh*.

We still had very little food. I remember looking at my sister and thinking, "She's like a skeleton. Do I look like that, too?" Whenever we found something, we gobbled it up till it was gone. There was no such thing as leftovers. At that time, we did not know that stuffing ourselves in our starved condition was dangerous. Some of the girls became bloated, and one of my best organizing friends died from overeating.

One morning another set of twins and I set off for the Vistula River, which was not far from camp. Armed with a couple of bottles and containers, we planned to crack the ice, lower the bottles, and fill them with fresh water.

As I stood on the bank of the river, I saw a girl my age on the other side. She had braided hair and wore a nice clean dress and a coat. On her back she carried a school bag, so I knew she was going to school.

I froze. I could not believe there was still a world out there where people were clean and girls wore braids with ribbons and nice dresses and went to school! Once, I had been that girl in nice clothes with ribbons in my hair on my way to school. Until that moment, I had thought everyone was in a concentration camp like us. But I realized then that was not true.

The girl stared at me. I looked down at myself wearing ragged clothes swarming with lice and a coat and shoes many sizes too big for me. I was hungry and scavenging for food and water. I do not know what she thought, but as I looked up again at her I could feel the fire of anger rising in me. I felt betrayed. Miriam and I had done nothing wrong! We were just little girls like her. Why were we in this situation while she was over there looking so pretty and clean and living a perfectly normal life? It was so wrong, so inconceivable to me. But there she was. And there I was.

After what seemed like a long time, she hitched up her book bag and walked away.

I stared after her, watching her leave, then watching the empty space where she had stood. I did not understand it. I could not understand it.

Then I felt a grumble in my stomach, reminding me of my hunger and thirst. I found a thick stick and jabbed it angrily against the surface of the icy river, cracking it until the hole was big enough. I lowered my bottle into the frozen river, turned it slightly sideways, and watched the bubbles of air escaping as it filled with clear river water. The image of the girl stayed in my mind—as did all my questions about the outside world.

When we had collected as much water as our bottles would hold, the twins and I returned to the camp. Once there, we made a small fire and boiled the water to kill any germs. Although we made the trip to the river a couple more times, I never saw the girl again.

We could not leave the camp because battles raged all around us. It was dangerous to wander outside. Guns fired indiscriminately and hit anyone in the way. We were in the middle of a battlefield. In the noise and confusion outside, we learned to dodge the *rat-a-tat-tat* of machine-gun fire. If we heard a certain whining sound, we had to run for cover because a bombshell was coming in our direction. Bursts of gunfire flashed and crackled from the bunkers where the SS had gone to hide after dropping us off at the barracks.

During those days, rumors spread that the whole camp was going to be blown up—the barracks, gas chambers, and crematorium—to cover up evidence of Nazi crimes. The SS forced sixty thousand prisoners to leave on a death march. Miriam and I and many of the twins stayed huddled in our lucky barracks. Thousands of other prisoners, too old and sick to march, also remained.

Later, I learned from an eyewitness account that, on the night of January 18, 1945, Dr. Mengele had paid one last call to the lab where we twins had been measured, injected, cut into, and bloodlet so many times. He took two boxes of papers containing records of the approximately three thousand twins he had experimented on at Auschwitz, stashed them in a waiting car, and drove off to join a group of fleeing Nazi soldiers.

For about nine days, we heard continuous shooting and bombing. The *boom-boom-boom* of artillery fire rattled the windows in our barracks. There was talk in the barracks among the adults that we were soon going to be set free. Liberation. Miriam and I did not know what that meant. We hid inside and waited.

On the morning of January 27, the noise stopped. For the first time in weeks, it was completely silent. We hoped this was liberation, but we had no idea what liberation would be like. Everyone in the barracks crowded at the windows.

It was snowing heavily. Until this day, I only remember the camp being gray—the buildings, streets, clothes, people—everything dirty and gray. In my mind, a constant smoky pall hung over the camp.

On this day, sometime late in the afternoon, maybe about 3 or 4pm, a woman ran to the front of the barracks and started yelling, "We are free! We are free! We are free!"

Free? What did she mean?

Everyone ran to the doorway. I stood on the top step, huge flakes of snow falling on me. I could not see anything beyond a few feet in front of me. The snow had fallen all day, and the dirty gray of Auschwitz was now covered in a white blanket of snow.

"Don't you see something coming?" asked an older girl.

I kept peering through the swirling snow. "No . . ." I squinted.

Then I saw them.

About twenty feet away, we saw Soviet soldiers emerging through the snow, approaching us in snow-covered capes and suits. They did not speak as they crunched through the snow.

As they came closer, they looked to us like they were smiling. Were those smirks or smiles? I peered closely. Yes, they were smiles. Real smiles. Joy and hope welled up inside of us. We were safe. We were free!

Crying and laughing, we ran up to the soldiers, crowding them.

A shout rose from the crowd: "We are free! We are free!" There was laughter and wails of relief all mixed together in a jumble of celebratory sounds.

Laughing themselves, some of them with tears in

their smiling eyes, the Soviet soldiers hugged us back. They handed us cookies and chocolate—delicious!

It was our first taste of freedom. And I realized that my silent pledge the first night in the latrine to survive and walk out of the camp alive with Miriam by my side had become a reality.

CHAPTER TEN

I threw my arms around the neck of a Soviet soldier, and he picked me up. I clung to him, with Miriam attached to my side. Everybody was hugging and kissing and shouting, "We are free!"

That night the soldiers continued the celebration in the barracks. They danced with the women and shared vodka with the men right out of the bottles. Everyone laughed and sang. There was music: people pounded homemade drums using spoons on food tins, and someone played an accordion. Some of the children joined in the dancing, jumping up and down on the floor, on the bunks, on the adults. I had never seen so much merriment, especially in our death camp.

Miriam and I sat happily on our bunk, watching and enjoying the scene of rare contentment and cheer. What a crazy sight. It was the pure human joy of being alive.

"We are free!" I mused aloud, nodding in time to the music.

"Yes. No more terrible *Pflegerinnen*!"

"No more *Heil, Doktor Mengele*!"

"No more experiments!"

"No more injections!"

"No more hangings."

"No more . . ."

We were having a contest to list everything we would *not* miss now that we were free.

"We can do what we want!" Miriam said, satisfaction filling her tiny face.

Her words stopped me short. *We can do what we want.*

I watched everyone celebrating, but did not see it. I heard the music and singing, but did not listen to it.

We can do what we want. Whatever we want. We are free.

Memories of home filled my eyes. The sounds of the farm echoed in my ears: chopping wood, chickens clucking, cows bellowing. The smells of ripe fruits in the orchards filled my nose. I have no idea how long I sat there thinking.

It was Miriam who interrupted my reverie. "What is it, Eva?" She shook my arm. "Eva! What?"

I turned to face her, my eyes finally adjusting to her presence. "Home," I stated. "I want to go home."

Miriam searched my face. "OK. We are free. Let's go home."

We took stock of our very few belongings, tucking them under us and into our clothing. That night we slept soundly for we had a plan: We were going home as soon as possible.

The following afternoon, many Soviet people gathered around us. They asked Miriam and me and all the surviving children, most of them twins, to put on striped prison uniforms over our clothes. Because we were Mengele's twins, we had never worn those Auschwitz uniforms before. I was already wearing two coats because it was so cold. Underneath our coats and dresses, Miriam and I carried everything we owned:

food, bowls, blankets—things we regarded as treasures.

We stood at the very head of the line and held hands as Soviet soldiers marched us out of the barracks between the high, barbed-wire fences. A nurse holding a small child in her arms walked beside us. Huge cameras kept filming, filming. I looked at the cameraman and wondered why he was taking our picture.

"Are we movie stars or something?" I wondered. I was very impressed with it all. The only real movies Miriam and I had seen were the ones starring Shirley Temple that our mama had taken us to in the city.

To my surprise, after we had all walked through the fences, the cameraman sent all of us back inside and directed us to march out again. With nuns, nurses, and Soviet soldiers accompanying us, rows and rows of twins filed back into the barracks, then right back out again. We repeated the action several times until the cameraman was satisfied. Years later, I found out that he wanted to capture the scene as part of a propaganda movie showing the world how the Soviet army had rescued Jewish children from the fascists.

The children at the front are Eva (left) and Miriam (right)

At last, for the final time, Miriam and I, hand in hand, walked out of the barracks in matching striped uniforms. Miriam and I had survived Auschwitz. We were eleven years old.

Now we had only one question: How exactly would we get home?

CHAPTER ELEVEN

All around us people were preparing to leave. They just walked away from camp. I did not know what direction to take. I did not know where on earth we were. In those days, I did not know there were countries called Poland and the Soviet Union. Having gone to school in a small village in Romania, I had learned nothing about the rest of the world.

For the next two weeks, Miriam and I stayed in Auschwitz with many other former prisoners. At first, we did not have enough to eat. I went back to the basement and filled my scarf with flour.

"*Nyet! Nyet!*" No! No! shouted a Soviet soldier. He fired a shot.

Frightened, I spilled the flour, ran outside, and raced back to Miriam. Later, I realized that the soldier was not shooting at me the way the Nazis had. He was trying to scare me. The Soviets had taken charge of the camp and were trying to maintain order.

I do not remember organizing any food after that. The Soviets fed us soup with beans in it that tasted good. As soon as Miriam and I started eating we could not stop. By then we knew that eating too much was bad for us, so Miriam and I monitored each other. We did not want to die from overeating like other twins we had known.

A few weeks later, we finally left Auschwitz. We were taken in a horse and wagon to an orphanage in a monastery in Katowice, Poland. Later we found out that the arrangements had been made by the Soviets, who were working with the Red Cross and Jewish refugee organizations.

When we arrived at the monastery, we were taken to our new living quarters. I was shocked. Miriam and I were given our own nice room. There were two beds with clean, white sheets. Sheets! I had not seen a white sheet in almost a year. I felt strange and out of place. No one had bothered to give us baths; we were filthy and covered with lice. There was no way I could sleep on that clean, white bed.

For a long time, I stared at the sheets. That night, I ripped them off the bed and went to sleep on the bare mattress. I did not want to make everything dirty. It seemed wrong.

The nuns had also put beautiful toys in our room, but the toys made me angry. Toys were for children. I was eleven years old, but I no longer knew how to play. What I wanted and needed was warmth and loving care. At Auschwitz, I had struggled to keep myself and Miriam alive. Now I only wanted to go home. The nuns did not know what to do with us. They considered us orphans.

I spoke up for Miriam and me. "We're twins. That's Miriam, and I am Eva Mozes. Our father is Alexander and our mother is Jaffa. We are from Portz." We spoke to them in Hungarian because we did not speak Polish; a translator then told them what we had said. Conversations took a long time.

"Where are your parents?" asked the nuns.

"I don't know."

"Who will take care of you?"

"I don't know. We want to go home," I kept telling them.

The nuns said, "Children cannot be released if they do not have parents."

"But we do have parents," I said.

"Where?"

"I have to go home to find out if they came back from the camp," I said. Now that we were safe, I could still hope to find Mama and Papa and my sisters.

The nuns told us we could not leave unless there was someone to take care of us. So there we had to stay.

I did not like living in a Catholic monastery. At this place, crosses, crucifixes, and paintings of the Virgin and Child surrounded us and seemed foreign. I longed for someplace more familiar. I wondered what my papa, a religious Jew, would think if he saw Miriam and me in a monastery. The nuns did not try to convert us or anything like that, but it was just so strange a place to find ourselves.

Older girls who had survived Auschwitz and were staying at the monastery told us that we could go into the town of Katowice and ride the streetcar without paying for tickets. All we had to do was show the numbers tattooed on our arms. They told us we did not have to speak Polish or say anything. Since we spoke mainly Hungarian, that was a small relief.

So we went into town and found what they told us was true: We could ride the streetcars for free. Over and over, Miriam and I rode the streetcar from one end of town to the other. The sheer joy of being free, feeling the wind in our ears, and being able to choose what we did was so liberating to us.

Through the older girls, we learned that some survivors of Auschwitz were being held in a displaced persons camp at Katowice, including our friend from home, Mrs. Csengeri, and her twin daughters. One day, I thought of a plan to get us out of the monastery.

"Come on, Miriam," I said. "We're going to see Mrs. Csengeri."

"Why?" asked Miriam.

"Just come with me."

We hopped on a streetcar and went to the camp. When we found Mrs. Csengeri, I began talking a mile a minute. "You were my mama's friend," I said. "We don't want to stay in the monastery, but they won't let us leave because we can't find our parents."

"Yes, I know," she replied. "But why are you telling me all this?"

I paused and then blurted, "Would you sign a paper saying you are our aunt and get us out so we can go home?"

At first, Mrs. Csengeri said nothing. Finally, she said, "OK. I will go to the monastery with you and sign the papers." She paused and then added, "And then I will take you home with me."

I was overjoyed.

In March 1945, Miriam and I moved into the camp with Mrs. Csengeri and her daughters. We lived in a room in the barracks and shared it with a lady, Mrs. Goldenthal, and her three children.

Mrs. Goldenthal's twin boys, Alex and Erno, were

our age, and I discovered that they had been selected at Auschwitz for Mengele's experiments like us. Mrs. Goldenthal had stayed with them, and I found out later that she had hidden a younger child, Margarita, underneath her long skirt. She had come into the camp with the child hidden in her dress and during her entire stay there, even in the Nazi barracks where she had kept Margarita under the mattress during inspections, she and the other women had helped conceal her child.

Now Mrs. Goldenthal and Mrs. Csengeri took care of all of us. They washed us and boiled our clothes. They got rid of the lice. Mrs. Csengeri sewed dresses for Miriam and me out of big Soviet khaki tunics. Wearing that dress made me feel like a little girl again. She even fixed special food for us. Miriam and I almost felt like a family again, being cared for by adults, the way it used to be.

The Soviet soldiers in charge of the camp gave us bread and a half a ruble every week to spend on anything we wanted. Sometimes, Miriam and I went to the outdoor market in town to buy an apple. Normally, we were given plain food that filled us, such as bread, potato soup, and meat. An apple was a luxury that we were thrilled to have.

One morning, after a month and a half, Mrs. Csengeri woke me up from a deep sleep. "Pack everything," she said, "because we're moving." We gathered our things together. Miriam and I, hand in hand in our matching khaki dresses, boarded a train with our small group. I had no idea where we were going, but we knew where we wished to go. All I wanted was to find my parents or somebody from my real family. All I wanted was to go home.

CHAPTER TWELVE

Soviet soldiers took charge as Miriam and I began the journey home with Mrs. Csengeri, Mrs. Goldenthal, and their children. Although we rode in a cattle car, it was very different from our ride to Auschwitz. The train was not crowded, and there were built-in bunk beds with little mattresses that were comfortable. We loved to sit on the top bunk bed and look out the windows, which this time were not covered by barbed wire. At night, we had as many blankets as we wanted. Miriam and I cuddled. We still did not talk about how we felt or what was going on. We just snuggled.

In the daytime, the doors of the train cars were left open. Often, Miriam and I sat in the doorway with our legs dangling out. The train lumbered along the tracks so slowly you could almost run alongside. The wind brushed our faces, and the fresh air felt wonderful. We enjoyed watching fields and hills slide by. It was spring. Flowers bloomed, birds chirped.

We were no longer in danger. We were free.

Sometimes the train stopped for five or six hours. We'd get off, and Mrs. Csengeri would set up two bricks, make a small fire, and cook something in a pot. The Soviets gave us bread and rations, but we had also taken along some food. I no longer had to worry about feeding us. Mrs. Csengeri took over and never complained. When the conductor called that the train was about to leave, we hopped on again.

We were heading toward Romania. On the train, we sang and talked. Mrs. Csengeri and Mrs. Goldenthal said they were going to save the striped prison uniforms they had worn at Auschwitz and testify to the world what had happened there. "I'll tell my story," Mrs. Csengeri kept saying. "I will tell what these monsters did to us." Back then, I did not understand why that was so important. I could not imagine who would want to hear about Auschwitz, but the women kept discussing

Rosie is in the middle. The twins, Yehudit and Lea, are on either side, and son Michael is being held by Zvi

it. The question came up as to whether their husbands had survived. I wondered if anybody in my family had survived besides Miriam and me. Nobody really knew.

Sometimes we passed through villages and towns that had been destroyed by bombing. Brick buildings lay in ruins. Rubble covered the ground. Some places seemed altogether abandoned. We went from Katowice in Poland to Czernowitz near the Romanian border. At the outer edge of the city, we stayed at a camp that may have been a labor camp or ghetto. We remained there for about two months and thought we were getting closer to home.

One afternoon, we were told to pack up, and we were loaded into another cattle car with bunk beds. As the train rumbled on, the grown-ups realized that we should have already reached Romania; Transylvania had become part of Romania again, it was no longer Hungary. Mrs. Csengeri watched the signs and said we were going deeper into the Soviet Union. When the train crawled uphill, some people jumped off and rolled away from the tracks. "Where are they going?" I wondered.

For years, I wondered what happened to them. Later, I realized that many people were frightened of the Soviet Union and did not want to live under communist rule.

After a week, we arrived at a refugee camp in Slutsk. It was close to Minsk in the Soviet Union. We lived there for a couple of months with former prisoners from all over Europe. Finally, we were grouped according to our home countries.

One day in October, we started back into Romania. Our first stop was Nagyvárad (Oradea), Mrs. Goldenthal's town. She and her children went home. I was so envious! I wanted to be back in our home! That night the rest of us stayed in a hotel near the train station and had dinner there. The food was very, very good, consisting of baked potatoes and fried eggs with seasoning, and apples and ice cream for dessert. For once, we were full after we ate. A Jewish agency gave us the money to pay our bill. Every town that had once had a Jewish population now had a Jewish agency to take care of displaced persons like us and help reunite families.

The next day, we boarded another train and rode

south to Șimleu Silvaniei, Mrs. Csengeri's town. She invited us to stay overnight. In the morning we thanked her for taking care of us and took the first train to Portz, our village.

When the train stopped and the conductor called, "Portz!" I immediately recognized the station. Holding hands, Miriam and I got off at the top of the hill and started down to the village. "Let's go home," I said. I had to see it. I am not sure what I expected to find. Would everything be the way we had left it, only maybe a little disheveled from the months we had been away? In my mind, home meant Miriam and me, our sisters and my parents, the farm and our animals. Any homecoming had to include at least some of these, right? I allowed myself to hope that there would be something good waiting for us.

Hand in hand, Miriam and I walked through the village. We were wearing our matching Soviet khaki tunic dresses, and I still had the shoes from the camp, twice the size of my feet. When I took a step, the front of the shoe flopped down first. People came out of their houses and whispered to each other. Nobody spoke to us directly. They just stared at us as we walked down the street. Miriam and I still looked alike. I had a feeling that the villagers knew who we were.

As we approached our house, my heart beat so hard I could hear it thumping. I could not wait to reach the gate. Finally—we would be home again! My memories of the house were of nice things and good times: warm beds and clothes that fit, a mother who cooked for us, a father who provided. My family.

But none of that was left. Nothing but the untilled land and the bare walls of an empty house.

Everything looked neglected. Abandoned. I realized immediately that Papa and Mama had not returned. They would never have let the weeds grow so high. They would never have let the house become run down.

It was at that moment that we knew, Miriam and I, that we were all that were left of the Mozes family. Grandma and Grandpa Hersh—our mother's primary reason for not escaping to Palestine—were also gone. There was nobody else.

Still holding hands, Miriam and I went inside. We were surprised when Mama's dog Lily, a little red Dachshund, ran out to greet us, barking and wagging her tail. All this time and there she was! She seemed to recognize us, and when we reached out to pet her, she licked our hands. I guess Jewish dogs were not taken to concentration camps, only Jewish people.

The house was dirty—and empty. Everything had been looted. Furniture, curtains, dishes, linens, candlesticks— everything. I walked from room to room searching for any reminders, any remnants of the life I had once lived. I found only three crumpled photographs wadded up on the floor. I picked them up and saved them.

One picture showed my older sisters, Edit and Aliz, with three of our cousins. Another was of Edit, Aliz, Miriam, and me and our teachers back in 1942. The third photo was the last picture of my whole family, taken in the autumn of 1943. In the black-and-white photograph, Miriam and I were wearing our matching burgundy dresses. This was the only proof I had that

Standing are cousin Magda, sister Edit, and cousin Aggi.
Lying on the grass are cousin Dvora and sister Aliz.
All the girls in this picture died in the camps.

once, not so long ago, I had a family. Miriam and I stayed for six or seven hours, roaming around the farm. The fruit trees were still there, and we ate some plums and apples, but villagers had picked most of the fruit. By mid-afternoon, our cousin Shmilu showed up. Aunt Irena, our father's youngest sister, had apparently sent word to him to come and get us. We later found out that she had traced us through the Red Cross. Miriam and I were among the last Jews to return to Transylvania, and Aunt Irena had continued to check lists to see if anyone from our family had survived. Thus she knew exactly when our train was due to arrive in Portz and had contacted Shmilu.

Shmilu was about twenty years old and had lived in a nearby village. He, too, had been imprisoned at Auschwitz and was the only one of his immediate family to survive. I told him the neighbors had stolen everything. "Yes," he said, "I know."

Shmilu had taken back a bed, a table, and a couple of chairs from the neighbors to fix up a room for himself in the summer kitchen of our farm. He was working the land and taking care of Lily. The dog wandered in and out, eating scraps around the farms.

We asked Shmilu questions about our parents. "I have not seen anyone from your family," he told us. "I know only that your Aunt Irena survived and is waiting for you." She had been sent to a concentration camp but had returned in May.

I did not feel comfortable in the house even though it was ours. I did not feel as though I belonged there any more. Miriam and I had no home, no parents, no sisters. But we still had each other.

We left with Cousin Shmilu. Villagers stood at their gates and silently watched us go. I was angry with them but said nothing. We boarded a train that would take Miriam and me to the big city of Cluj to join our aunt.

We would make a new life for ourselves somehow.

CHAPTER THIRTEEN

For the next five years, from 1945 to 1950, Miriam and I lived with Aunt Irena. She owned a large apartment house in Cluj.

Before the war, Miriam and I had always enjoyed visits to Aunt Irena's home and her visits to see us. She and her husband traveled extensively, and she would tell us stories of vacations on the French Riviera and Monte Carlo. We loved to hear about and see her jewelry and furs. Her son was our favorite cousin.

But a year or two after our arrival in Cluj, we began to discover that freedom was not what we had thought it would be. Romania was now controlled by the communists. The Communist Party was the only political party and had complete power. The secret police force arrested anyone opposed to the government and took over people's property and gave it to the peasants.

During the war, the Nazis had forced Aunt Irena to work in a bomb factory in Germany. Her husband and son had perished in the camps. When she returned to Cluj, she found that the communists had taken most of her possessions. However, the state let Aunt Irena keep her building because she was a war widow and a survivor of the concentration camps. She married a pharmacist who was also a survivor.

We all lived together, but we were not really a family. We knew our aunt cared about us because she was the only one of our relatives willing to take us in. But Aunt Irena never hugged or kissed us, or spoke kindly. Miriam and I hungered for affection and yearned for a loving mother.

Aunt Irena still had Persian rugs, a porcelain collection, and some designer clothes left from her prewar days. These treasures reminded her of the good life she used to have and, strangely, seemed to mean more to her than we did.

Miriam and I felt out of place in that grand apartment. We were sloppy and messy. We were eleven-year-old kids who had returned from the barracks of Auschwitz. We did not belong in Auschwitz, but we did not entirely belong in this fancy apartment in Cluj, either.

Every night, I had nightmares. I dreamed of rats the size of cats, dead bodies, and needles stuck into me. After we found out that the Nazis had made soap out of Jewish fat, I dreamed that soap bars spoke to me in the voices of my parents and sisters, asking me, "Why are you washing with us?"

I did not tell Miriam because I was afraid I would make her feel bad and give her nightmares, too. We both developed health problems and caught colds all the time. Painful sores covered our bodies. The sores grew as big as apples and formed scars. When Aunt Irena took us to the doctor, I was terrified—I remembered Dr. Mengele and his assistants in white coats. I had learned not to trust doctors so much.

After the Romanian doctor had examined us, he said, "These children have what many war children are suffering from: malnutrition. There is nothing wrong with them that vitamins and a good diet cannot fix."

At that time, vitamins were not available and food was scarce. We stood in line for hours to get a loaf of bread. Our cousin Shmilu brought flour, potatoes, eggs, vegetables, and sunflower oil from the farm. Miriam and I craved that oil and drank it straight from the bottle! This worried Aunt Irena, but the doctor told her to let us drink it, that we seemed to be getting better.

One day, as I was eating white bread on the veranda of the apartment, someone saw me and reported me to the secret police. That night the police came and raided the apartment and seized all our food. The next day, my aunt built a fake cabinet that looked like a wall. You could only get in there by pushing a button. From then on, we hid our food in the cabinet.

One night, the secret police picked up Aunt Irena's husband without any explanation. He disappeared. We did not know whether he was alive or dead. When we walked outside, we always worried who was watching or listening. Someone might turn us in to the secret police.

Life in communist Romania became more and more difficult. The government controlled everything, including schools. On the first day of high school, Miriam and I wore our matching khaki dresses. We remembered going to school in Portz in our matching burgundy dresses. Now all the children made fun of us because of our clothes. We had only missed a year and a half and were not far behind in our studies. School, however, was harder for us because we spoke Hungarian, and classes were taught in Romanian.

At school, we were the only Jews. Other students called us names despite what we had been through. Anti-Semitic people in Cluj spread rumors that at night a Jewish vampire stalked Christian girls and sucked their blood. Miriam and I went to an orphanage for our evening meal since there wasn't enough food at Aunt Irena's. As we walked home, I kept thinking, "How will this vampire know I am Jewish and not attack me?"

But it was not just the Jews who were being persecuted. Conditions were terrible for everyone. Eventually, Miriam and I went to a Jewish Zionist organization to

Eva and Miriam as high-school students in Cluj

learn about Palestine, but the government later shut the organization down. Sometimes we received packages from our aunt in the United States. Once she sent some fabric, and Aunt Irena took us to the seamstress and had three sets of matching dresses made for Miriam and me. Our favorite was blue with little polka dots. We loved wearing matching dresses to attract attention and fool the boys. Our American aunt also sent coats, but they were adult styles and did not fit.

One day in 1948, when we were fourteen, the government announced that the store would have new coats for sale. Miriam and I stood in line all night waiting for the store to open at ten o'clock in the morning. But twelve thousand people showed up—for two hundred coats! When the doors opened and people rushed in, a saleslady who was a friend of our aunt's recognized us. She threw us two coats and shoved us under a counter. Later on, we paid for them and walked out with matching rust-colored coats, the color of autumn leaves. We wore those coats when we sailed to Israel much later.

Palestine became the State of Israel in 1948. I began

to think it would be a privilege to live in a place where my father had dreamed of living. The last time we had seen Papa, he had made us promise that, if we survived, we would go to Palestine.

Miriam and I exchanged letters with Uncle Aaron, our papa's brother, who lived in Haifa, and we sent him a picture of us. Uncle Aaron offered to help us resettle and ease our suffering. We wrote him and asked if there was chocolate in Israel. He replied, telling us that we could eat all the chocolate we wanted and all the oranges we wanted, too. He would take care of us. We thought Israel sounded like paradise!

Aunt Irena said she had received news that her son was alive and living in Israel. She wanted to emigrate, too. We all applied for exit visas, and our aunt's was granted easily. It took Miriam and me two years to obtain ours. The government did not want to let young people leave Romania because they needed the youth to rebuild the war-ravaged country.

Nevertheless, we started preparing for our trip. The rules changed daily about what we could take. We packed one year before we left and lived surrounded by boxes filled with things we wanted to bring. In order to leave the country, Miriam and I had to sign over our remaining property. We still owned two acres of farmland and the house in Portz. The communists had already claimed most of the farm to divide among the peasants. We wanted to leave so badly, we signed it over.

Two months before we left Romania, Aunt Irena's husband was released from prison and given a visa. He did not say a word to us girls about what had happened to him. We were just glad he had been freed.

Finally, in June 1950, when we were about to leave, the government informed us that all we could take with us was only what we could wear. The day we left, Aunt Irena made us put on three dresses underneath our matching coats. I carefully wrapped the creased photos of my family in paper and brought them with me.

We took a train to Constanța, a city on the coast of the Black Sea. Pushing and shoving, we lined up to board the ship. Miriam and I were squashed. I could hardly breathe. But we tightly clutched each other's hands so that we would not be separated. There were three thousand people on a ship built to hold only a thousand. We waited for twenty-four hours before we set sail.

As we pulled away from shore, I knew there was nothing left for Miriam and me in Romania. During the past five years I had continued to hope that our sisters or parents might come back. The Jewish organizations working with the Red Cross had posted lists of people returning. I had checked the lists at the orphanage where we ate dinner every night, but there was no sign of any member of my family. Miriam and I were sixteen years old. We needed to move on.

It was a long, tiring trip. For days and days, we saw no land but it was exciting to be on the open sea. The endless stretch of water and sky, with fresh air and the wind sifting through our hair, smelled of freedom and promise. Hand in hand, Miriam and I watched dolphins jumping in and out of the ocean.

Early one morning, our ship approached Haifa. As the boat docked, we stood on the deck and watched the sun rise over Mount Carmel, Israel. It was one of the most beautiful sights I had ever seen. The land of freedom. Most of the passengers on the ship were Holocaust survivors like us. Everybody burst into the Israeli national anthem, "Hatikvah." We were crying and singing with joy.

As we disembarked at the port, we searched for a person looking for us. Uncle Aaron finally spotted us, yelling our names and waving his arms so we would be sure to see him. We hugged, and he kissed us. We cried in his arms. It had been so long since my sister and I had received any real love from anyone besides each other.

My twin sister and I, in our matching rust-colored coats and layers of matching dresses, felt at last that we had come home.

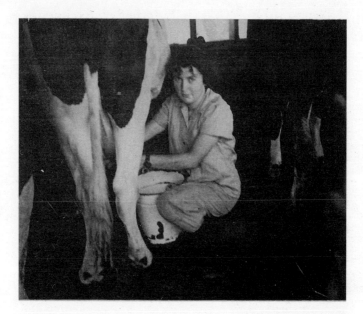

Eva milking a cow

CHAPTER FOURTEEN

When we arrived in Haifa with Uncle Aaron, we learned that Aunt Irena's son was not there after all. She had made up the story to get a visa. Miriam and I were sad to realize that our favorite cousin was actually gone forever. We spent the afternoon with Uncle Aaron and his family. It was agreed that Miriam and I would go to one of the Youth Aliyah Villages that had been set up by the Israeli government. The villages were located on huge farms where young people like us planted and harvested crops and tended the animals. The food we produced helped feed the new nation of Israel.

At our village, we worked half the day and went to school half the day. My jobs were to pick tomatoes and peanuts and milk cows.

Miriam and I were at the village with about three

hundred other teenagers from many different countries. Not all of the youth were Holocaust survivors like us. Some kids lived at the village while their parents trained for jobs. We were all put into groups upon arrival and would become friends. Each dormitory had a housemother, but we would take care of our own rooms. For the first time since leaving Auschwitz, I would sleep without having nightmares. I would no longer have to worry about our physical safety or survival. There was no anti-Semitism, and we would be allowed, indeed encouraged, to celebrate our Jewish heritage. Our hurts and suffering would slowly begin to heal in those youth villages.

Although we all arrived speaking a variety of languages, we were taught a common language: Hebrew. I learned a few words the very first night Miriam and I spent at the village. It was a Friday. That night and every Friday night, all the kids gathered in a huge dining room to welcome the *Shabbat*, the Jewish Sabbath. There were candles and wine on the tables. We all wore white shirts. Two girls were assigned to Miriam and me as "big sisters" and made us feel at home.

After prayers, everyone started singing and dancing the *hora*. But I did not know how. "Can I do this dance?" I wondered. My big sister took my hand, Miriam's big sister grasped hers, as everyone joined hands and formed a circle. We danced to the right. I did not know the steps but I followed along. With arms raised high we danced together, boys and girls, all of us singing "Hava Nagila." Laughing, we danced round and round, faster and faster. I danced the *hora* and was filled with joy. Miriam and I were finally part of a new, large, welcoming family.

EVA'S EPILOGUE

Eva Mozes Kor, April 2009

In Israel we lived for two years in the Youth Village. We went to school half the day and worked on the farm for the other half. We learned Hebrew quickly, within two years rapidly skipping up from one class to the next, finally finishing in the tenth grade. Miriam worked in the field, and I was a milkmaid. I was the only girl working with six guys. I learned to say "I love you" in ten different languages, which, at age sixteen, seemed like an important thing to know.

In 1952, we were drafted into the Israeli army, where Miriam studied nursing and became a registered nurse. I studied drafting and became a draftsperson, someone who draws plans of buildings or machines. I was stationed in Tel Aviv and stayed in the Israeli army for eight years, reaching the rank of sergeant major.

Those years were growing years for me. I became a very good draftswoman and I learned that I was able to earn a living. But I longed for a home and a family of my own.

In April 1960, I met an American tourist, Michael Kor, who was visiting his brother in Tel Aviv. Even though we could hardly communicate, we got married a few weeks later. He had said something to me in English; that night I had looked it up and replied, "Yes." It was a marriage proposal. The next thing I knew, I was a married woman living in Terre Haute, Indiana, where Michael had lived since 1947. He had come there after the war specifically to live close to his liberator from the US Allied Forces. Let me tell you that it is not a particularly good idea to marry someone without being able to communicate in the same language. Both of us had too many surprises to contend with while getting to know one another. For instance, he initially thought I was a very quiet person! As you might have figured out from this memoir, I am not; it was simply that I could not speak any English.

Coming from Tel Aviv to Terre Haute was like

landing on the moon. I knew nothing about life in the United States, spoke no English, and thought everyone was rich. Within a few weeks, I got pregnant. I was so very homesick, missing Miriam and my friends in Israel, that I watched TV to drown out my loneliness. At the time, I thought that all that Americans showed on TV were news and sports, because those were the only two kinds of programs that my husband watched.

One day, to my surprise, there was a movie on TV about a young couple dating, kissing, and living like young people do. Now this was a TV show worth watching! I became engrossed in the show, looking away from the action only to jot down words I did not know so I could later look them up in the dictionary. I then proceeded to memorize those words. In this way, I learned to speak English well enough to get a job within three months of my arrival to the States.

Our son, Alex Kor, was born on April 15, 1961, and our daughter, Rina Kor, on March 1, 1963. I thought my life was complete. But still, my childhood experiences continued to come back to haunt me. The birthday

Top row (l to r): Eva, Mickey Kor, Mickey's niece Miri, brother Shlomo, and sister-in-law Sara. In front is Mickey's nephew AuShalom.

parties started, which became a problem because my toddlers asked me how come they had no grandparents like all their friends did.

When Alex was six years old, on Halloween a very popular kid and his friends came over to play tricks on my son. Those tricks reminded me of the days when the Nazi youth harassed us in Portz, days when I was helpless and could do nothing to defend myself. But this time I lived in this great country where I did not have to put up with it! So I went outside and chased those kids away. Because of this I became very "popular" with the kids at Halloween. Every year, the harassment would begin on October 1: They painted swastikas on our home and put white crosses in the yard—it was awful.

Alex would come home from school crying and saying, "Mom, I'm so ashamed of you! All the kids say that you are crazy! Why can't you be like all the other mothers?" I told my son that I was not crazy, but neither was I like all the other mothers. I thought that if I could tell the story of what had happened to me as a child, the kids would understand and leave me alone to live in peace in my home. But as a victim of such atrocities, I did not know how to accomplish this.

I was harassed for eleven years, until 1978 when NBC aired the show "Holocaust." Suddenly, everybody understood why I was different. Those same kids who had taunted me at Halloween called me or wrote to me to apologize. I began lecturing in 1978, and people always asked me about the details of the experiments. I never knew all the details about Auschwitz, but I thought that there would be lots of information available about the camps and about Dr. Mengele. Unfortunately, I could not find any information in any book. I remembered that in the liberation film, about two hundred children were shown marching out of the camp. If I could contact those children, now adults, we could share our memories and piece together what had been done to us. But I didn't know where to find them.

It took me six years to come up with the idea of forming an organization to help me and Miriam locate the Mengele twins. In 1984, we founded CANDLES, an acronym for Children of Auschwitz Nazi Deadly Lab

Eva and Miriam at Auschwitz, 1991

Eva holding unused vials of substances used in
Dr. Mengele's experiments. The content of the vials
is unknown; they have never been opened or tested.

Experiments Survivors. We located 122 survivors living in ten countries and on four continents. CANDLES, as a support group, helped many twins deal with some of the special issues that we all had as survivors of Mengele's experiments.

As time went on, Miriam had more and more problems with her kidneys. We knew it had something to do with the injections she had been given in Auschwitz, but we never found out what it was that prevented her kidneys from growing beyond the size of a ten-year-old's. By 1987, her kidneys failed. I donated my left kidney, which helped her live until June 6, 1993. We never did find out what she or any of us had been injected with. I am still searching and hoping to discover this information.

Miriam's death was devastating to me. I knew that I had to do something positive in her memory. So in 1995 I opened the CANDLES Holocaust Museum and Education Center, in Terre Haute, Indiana. Over fifty thousand people have visited the museum since we opened its doors, most of them young people.

In 1993, I traveled to Germany and met with a Nazi doctor from Auschwitz, Dr. Münch. Surprisingly, he was very kind to me. Even more surprising, I found that I liked him. I asked him if he knew anything about the gas chambers in Auschwitz. He said that what he knew had been fueling the nightmares he lived with every single day. He went on to describe it, saying, "People would be told they were taking a shower and to remember their clothes hanger number, and to tie their shoes together. When the gas chamber was fully packed, the doors closed hermetically and sealed. A vent-like orifice opened in the ceiling, dropping pellets like gravel to the floor. Somehow the pellets operated like dry ice and turned to gas. The gas began rising from the floor. People tried to get away from the rising gas, climbing on top of one another. The strongest people ended atop a pile of intermingled bodies. When the people on the top of the pile stopped moving, that was when I knew, from looking through a peephole and watching it all, that everybody was dead." Dr. Münch signed the mass death certificates; there were no names on them, just

From middle left, Rina Kor (holding document), Alex Kor,
Eva Mozes Kor, and Dr. Münch at Auschwitz in 1993
signing their statements

that there were two thousand or three thousand dead people.

I told Dr. Münch that this was very important information, for I had not known that the gas chambers worked that way. I asked him if he would come with me to Auschwitz in 1995, when we would be celebrating the fiftieth anniversary of our liberation from the camp. I further asked him to sign an affidavit about what he had said and seen and done, and to do it at the site of all those killings. He said that he would love to.

So I returned from Germany, and I was so glad that I would have an original document witnessed and signed by a Nazi—a participator, not a survivor and not a liberator—to add to the historical collection of information we were preserving for ourselves and for future generations. I was so grateful that Dr. Münch was willing to come with me to Auschwitz and sign that document about the operation of the gas chambers, and I wanted to thank him. But what does one give a Nazi doctor? How can one thank a Nazi doctor?

For ten months, I pondered this question. All kinds

of ideas popped into my head until I finally thought: "How about a simple letter of forgiveness from me to him? Forgiving him for all that he has done?" I knew immediately that he would appreciate it, but what I discovered once I made the decision was that forgiveness is not so much for the perpetrator, but for the victim. I had the power to forgive. No one could give me this power, and no one could take it away. That made me feel powerful. It made me feel good to have any power over my life as a survivor.

I began writing my letter and came up with several versions, working through a lot of pain. Concerned about my spelling, I called my former English professor to correct my letter. We met a few times, and she asked me to think about forgiving Dr. Mengele as well. At first I was shocked, but later I promised her that I would, for I realized that I had the power even to forgive the Angel of Death. "Wow," I thought, "it makes me feel good that I can do that. I have that power, and I am not hurting anyone with it."

We arrived in Auschwitz in January 27, 1995. Dr.

Münch came with his son, daughter, and granddaughter, and I came with my son, Alex Kor, and my daughter, Rina. Dr. Münch signed his document. Then I read my own personal statement of forgiveness, and I signed it.

Immediately, I felt that a burden of pain had been lifted from my shoulders, a pain I had lived with for fifty years: I was no longer a victim of Auschwitz, no longer a victim of my tragic past. I was free. I also took that moment to forgive my parents, whom I had hated all my life for not protecting us from Auschwitz, for not saving us from growing up as orphans. I finally understood that they had done the best that they could. I also forgave myself for hating my parents in the first place.

Anger and hate are seeds that germinate war. Forgiveness is a seed for peace. It is the ultimate act of self-healing.

I look at forgiveness as the summit of a very tall mountain. One side is dark, dreary, wet, and very difficult to climb. But those who struggle up and reach the summit can see the beauty of the other side of the mountain, which is covered in flowers, white doves, butterflies, and sunshine. Standing at the summit we can see both sides of the mountain. How many people would choose to go back down on the dreary side rather than stroll through the sunny flower-covered side?

I have given over three thousand speeches throughout the world, written two books, and contributed three chapters in three other books. I hope to teach young people the life lessons I have learned through all my pain and everything I have been through and survived:

1. Never ever give up on yourself or your dreams, for everything good in life is possible.
2. Judge people on their actions and the content of their character.
3. Forgive your worst enemy and forgive everyone who has hurt you—it will heal your soul and set you free.

When I look back on my teenage years, I would never have believed that anyone would want to listen to me or that I would have anything important to say. So I am saying to you, whoever is reading this book, to remember: never ever give up. You can survive and make your dreams come true.

And I would like to end with a quote from my Declaration of Amnesty read at the fiftieth anniversary of the liberation of Auschwitz:

I hope, in some small way, to send the world a message of forgiveness; a message of peace, a message of hope, a message of healing.

Let there be no more wars, no more experiments without informed consent, no more gas chambers, no more bombs, no more hatred, no more killing, no more Auschwitzes.

AFTERWORD

Peggy Tierney, April 2020

Eva Kor's memoir was first published in 2009, and Lisa Rojani Buccieri captured Eva's voice and story as she wanted it to be told. The first-person narrative provides insight into what Eva was thinking and feeling, but it doesn't necessarily convey what it was like to know Eva, the events in the last ten years of her life, and the stories behind the stories, both positive and negative.

Eva—and she always told everyone to call her Eva—was a tiny woman. At the end of her life, she was four feet nine inches, but she stood out in any crowd, always decked out in her signature look: the Eva Kor blue pantsuit. She changed it up by wearing different scarves or a printed blouse topped with a blue vest, but it was always a particular bright blue. She said, "I am somebody because of who I am inside, and no outfit can change that. I do like to look good, and I like blue because I like the way it looks on me, and it makes it simpler to dress, like a uniform. I don't have to waste any more time and effort on it. I do not like to wear black, my topic is too dark, and I like to liven up my appearance."

If the book gives readers the impression that Eva could be stubborn, singled-minded, willing to do or say something people might not like, that was true to life. Those very qualities enabled Eva and Miriam's survival in Auschwitz. Eva acknowledged that her father's harshness prepared her for the camp; likewise, her parents' secrecy and denials made Eva realize that adults don't always tell the truth, making her less likely to believe anything the Nazis said, which saved Eva and Miriam's lives more than once. As an adult, she was opinionated and direct, at times combative. But she always said, "Don't make me a saint. Don't put me on a pedestal. I don't want the pressure." To hear her speak, to hear her story and lessons, and to witness the magnitude of her generosity and her tireless efforts to help people from all walks of life, it was hard not to put her on a pedestal. But she was right to avoid sainthood. She showed us that it doesn't take a saint to forgive enemies, to be a champion, and to try to bring transformative peace and kindness to the world.

When Eva discovered the power of forgiveness to heal the decades of pain she had suffered from the Holocaust, the primary audience with whom she hoped to share her experience was other Holocaust survivors. Both before and after her forgiveness, she was a relentless advocate for survivors and Holocaust-related concerns. She was a catalyst in the movement to pressure governments worldwide to uncover and prosecute Nazis war criminals, responsible for millions of deaths, who were living freely, mostly in Europe or South America. She joined in the pursuit of financial justice for Holocaust survivors, and particularly for the Mengele twins. The twins received an apology from the Kaiser Wilhelm Institute (in 1943, Dr. Mengele had started sending specimens from Auschwitz to the KWI forAnthropology, Human Heredity and Eugenics in Berlin), and a lawsuit against the chemical company

Bayer, which used Jewish slave labor during the war, was incorporated into a class action, which ended with a German settlement fund that made payments to survivors. She advocated for laws mandating Holocaust education in US public schools, and she used her speaking fees to sponsor educators to attend her group trips to Auschwitz, so that they, in turn, could teach the Holocaust with more depth and insight. In a public statement on her forgiveness, Eva said:

> Many people hold onto pain and anger. Unfortunately, this does not help the survivors, and that is my only focus. My forgiveness has nothing to do with the perpetrators. It is an act of self-healing, self-liberation, and self-empowerment. It's free, it has no side effects, and it works. I highly recommend that everyone try it.

Eva's forgiveness message was not universally well received, particularly in the beginning. Most survivors were offended, understandably, at hearing that Eva had forgiven the Nazis. It sounded to them like Eva had forgiven the Nazis on behalf of all survivors, when they did not want anyone to forgive the Nazis, much less on their behalf. It was an unfortunate misunderstanding, because from the day that Eva read her "Declaration of Amnesty" at Auschwitz, saying, "I, Eva Mozes Kor, in my name only," she always stressed that forgiveness is a personal decision for individuals to make only for themselves, on their own timeline. She never meant for her forgiveness to be a blanket forgiveness on anyone's behalf but her own. Many survivors felt some things were simply too bad to forgive, and the Holocaust was in that category. It is not difficult to understand a view of the Holocaust as unforgiveable; its existence testifies to the outer limits of cruelty, greed, and hatred.

Another major factor that caused rejection of Eva's forgiveness lay in its definition; forgiveness was a word that Eva had redefined. Eva knew what she had done was not forgiveness in the traditional sense. Traditional forgiveness involves atonement and reconciliation between someone who has been hurt and the person who hurt them. There was no reconciliation or atonement found in Eva's forgiveness, and she considered justice a separate issue. She said, "I knew using the word 'forgiveness' in the way I was using it would cause confusion. I tried to think of another word, but no perfect term occurred to me. So I kept using the word 'forgiveness,' but I hoped I could explain to people what I meant and they would warm up to it." Unfortunately, that did not always happen. She often became frustrated with survivors who she felt were suffering needlessly, sometimes coming across as berating them or even criticizing them for not trying her forgiveness—unfairly, as her son, Alex, acknowledged. That also caused some to question her motivations.

One of the biggest moments of controversy surrounding Eva was when she traveled to Germany to attend the trial of Oskar Gröning, known as the "accountant of Auschwitz." She had written a letter to Gröning beforehand, in which she said:

It is true, but sad, that we cannot change what

happened in Auschwitz. I am hoping that you and I, as former adversaries, can meet as people who respect one another as human beings and can relate to one another to understand, to heal, and to express thoughts that would not be possible any other way. Any time adversaries meet to repair a relationship, they learn a great deal about themselves and how people function. It cannot be done on television, by telephone, or by Skype; it can only be done face to face.

I am one of the Auschwitz survivors who has chosen to participate as a co-plaintiff in your case, and I am probably the only survivor who has forgiven all the Nazis, including you, in my name alone. My forgiveness does not absolve the perpetrators from taking responsibility for their actions, nor does it diminish my need and right to ask questions about what happened at Auschwitz.

Eva was aware that Gröning had acknowledged his role in the Holocaust and expressed remorse. He had publicly spoken out on the activities in the camp, exposing the lies of Holocaust deniers as a personal witness to Nazi atrocities. Eva believed Gröning deserved punishment, but felt that a sentence requiring him to speak about his experiences to students would contribute more to public good than sentencing him to jail. Eva felt that the trial should be more about healing of Nazi victims and prevention of neo-fascism.

At the end of the hearing's first day, Eva wanted talk to Gröning. When she arrived, he became emotional and tried to get up, but collapsed, sliding down from his wheelchair. Eva grabbed his feet, and her lawyer, Markus Goldbach, held his upper body to stop his fall and avoid injury until the court marshals arrived to help.

Eva testified the next morning, reading her statement about her forgiveness and her thoughts on his punishment. At the lunch break, Eva approached Gröning to shake his hand and tell him how important it was that he would speak the truth as he did in the past. As Goldbach described it: "In a spontaneous gesture, Gröning pulled Eva slightly down and gave her a kiss on the cheek, overwhelmed with emotion." Eva was surprised but could not react, especially as she was so small. Eva and her lawyer both felt that he was not just grateful for Eva's ideas on his punishment but also moved by Eva's testimony of her suffering. Goldbach noticed that when Gröning was testifying, he was switching between past and present, and it appeared that some part of him had never really left Auschwitz.

Gröning's kiss became a photograph published by media around the world, and it added to the image of Eva as a friend to the Nazis. Articles about the trial and the photograph included Eva's forgiveness, but rarely indicated that she had appeared to provide testimony that would help to convict Gröning, and did not attempt to clarify what she meant by forgiveness.

Gröning and Eva's post-hearing kiss did indeed upset many survivors. For most people who read or watched the news stories, important context was lacking. Gröning's actions after the war create a somewhat more understandable picture of Eva's acceptance of a spontaneous gesture of gratitude from a repentant, elderly man. Unfortunately for Eva, like Dr. Hans Münch, Gröning did not have any first-hand information on the medical experiments.

Eva's compassion extended to the people of Germany as well. During the writing of this book, she insisted that soldiers at Auschwitz not be referred to as German soldiers, but as Nazi soldiers. She knew that not all Germans were Nazis. She did not believe in inherited guilt and felt that to impose guilt on German people who were not even alive during Word War II, much less involved in the Holocaust, was unfair. She shared a story:

In 2005 I went to Germany with a friend, a German lady whose name is Gunda. I met Gunda in 2000 when she invited me to lecture at her school in Rockford, Illinois. She never liked to deal with World War II, nor the Holocaust. Since she was a little girl, she had been called a Nazi because she was German, but she was born after the war and knew nothing about the Nazis. She tried to stay as far away from the stories of the Holocaust as she could, but a teacher colleague encouraged her to invite me anyway. I was different, a survivor who had forgiven the Nazis.

When I met Gunda, I told her that she didn't have to feel guilty for being born German, and she was only responsible for her own actions. We became very good friends, and she decided to go with me to Germany—I was the keynote speaker at conference run by Albrecht and Brigitte Mahr. "I had a great response after I spoke at the conference, and I was scheduled to conduct a three-hour workshop. Frankly, I was concerned what I could do with fifty people, to keep them busy and involved for three hours. As we were walking, a lady speaking English approached and introduced herself as Renee Levi, a child of a Holocaust survivor. She asked me if I knew any children of Nazis. I said, "Yes, Renee, meet Gunda." We ate lunch together, and they could not stop talking. There was a deep connection between those two.

When I started my workshop, I thought that having Renee and Gunda share their stories and their emotional connection was an important way of showing how two children of former enemies connected. Then when I was readying to begin the workshop, ten people came up to me; they also wanted to share their thoughts. Then forty people came up to me to share their experiences and thoughts, and then three hours had passed, and that was the workshop.

I learned that day the Germans carry a great deal of pain with them; four women had told of avoiding having babies because they did not want to have another generation of Germans feeling guilty for being Germans. The guilt and scars left on Germans for being German is difficult to understand, but it's there for many.

Eva was contacted by a German man, Michael Wörle, who was the grandson of Otmar von Verschuer, the mentor of Nazi Dr. Josef Mengele. Dr. von Verschuer was with the Kaiser Wilhelm Institute in Berlin, where he developed and directed the twin experiments conducted in Auschwitz. Dr. von Verschuer's family had not known or acknowledged his work for the Nazis and his role in the Auschwitz experiments. After Wörle came across some of his grandfather's writings that he found disturbing, he researched more deeply. After his research led to the difficult truth, he reached out to Eva. They became fast friends, and Wörle accompanied Eva on her trips to Germany, helping with travel and meeting arrangements and acting as a guide and translator.

In 2014, on the annual trip to Auschwitz, the group with Eva noticed another group, made up of German high-school girls, at the cattle car on the selection platform. She approached them on the spot, as they were obviously distressed and emotional, with tears and red cheeks, and even more so when she told them she had been a prisoner there when she was ten years old. She then spoke to them kindly, giving each of them a hug, telling them, "You don't have to feel guilty. You didn't do this. You weren't even born. But what you do have is a responsibility to remember and share what you've seen. Be a witness, prevent this from ever happening again. Your duty is to go make the world a better place." The tour group watched the girls' tears turn into smiles, a special moment for everyone who witnessed it.

Eva was accused more than once of trying to start controversy in order to get attention. In general, it is almost impossible to avoid controversy when advocating for change, and Eva's redefinition of forgiveness was radical. While many felt that forgiveness should not occur without the victimizer asking for forgiveness and offering atonement for that forgiveness, Eva always responded to this line of thought by pointing out that requirement allows the victimizer to retain control over the victim. Nazis were either dead or hiding, or denying their role in the war. In her view, she or any other survivor would be doomed to a life of anger and suffering if they were required to wait for an apology that would never come. Eva insisted that the right to be happy, to be free from pain, should be viewed as a universal human right.

As for her desire for attention, when Eva did get the spotlight, she used it, as she always did, to educate people on the Holocaust and the use of forgiveness to bring happiness and peace to the world. Holding up two fingers in the classic peace sign became the signature Eva pose seen in many photographs, particularly near the end of her life.

Not all survivors felt alienated by Eva's actions. She had friendships with a number of fellow survivors who did not agree with her forgiveness but shared the bond of the Holocaust and their Jewish heritage, and respected her tireless work in Holocaust education. One survivor even found the courage to return to Auschwitz for the first time in the company of Eva. Many survivors of the Holocaust and other genocides came to the museum in Terre Haute, Indiana, to speak. For survivors in need, Eva was quick to provide emotional and financial support. It's also worth noting that two of the world's top Holocaust experts engaged with Eva. Rabbi Michael Berenbaum did not believe that Eva's forgiveness met the requirements of Jewish law, but he respected her

efforts to provide Holocaust education. USC Shoah
Foundation Director Stephen D. Smith chose to include
Eva as one of the survivors in their Dimensions in
Testimony program to share her Auschwitz experience
and present her ideas of forgiveness, though he himself
felt that determining who or what is forgivable to be a
personal decision.

When Eva urged young people to "use their beautiful
minds," another of her life lessons, she was drawing from
her own past, when she sometimes took years to come
up with solutions or answers that she needed. She never
stopped thinking, she never stopped questioning, she
never stopped her mental examination of life, of people,
of her own story, of forgiveness, of humans in general—
what motivates them and what helps them.

Eva's daily life was infused by her sense of mission,
with a single-mindedness that is rare to find. Unless
she had an engagement elsewhere, she showed up at
her museum to lead tours and give talks to groups—
especially schoolchildren. She also read all the emails
she received, responding to questions, and giving advice,

words of comfort, and words of encouragement to those who were struggling with issues in their own lives.

The best days at the museum were those when she had school groups. Children and teens responded to Eva because she spoke to them honestly, never speaking down to them. So often, adults think of childhood as a carefree period, but in fact many children have unimaginably difficult lives, as Eva did herself. Eva also acknowledged that growing up is difficult, even in the best of circumstances. She spoke to children and teens as intelligent human beings, with respect and understanding of the challenges in their lives, and they loved her for it. At her events, she made time for all who approached her.

One would think that a person who had been treated so cruelly by so many people in her life would be distrustful, would have a wall, a tough outer layer. But that was one of the contradictions of her character. She could be tough. She was a sergeant major in the Israeli army, and that sometimes became apparent. But she was amazingly open, and, with the exception of young people wearing distressed jeans—her pet peeve—she welcomed everyone into the museum, on her trips, and into her group of supporters.

Her list of life lessons continued to grow, beyond the basics listed in the Epilogue. One of the last ones she added was "Be yourself, just be the best you that you can be."

Eva was true to her advice. She owned herself, from her age, her gender, her religion and her background to her Eva-blue polyester pantsuits, her hatred of ripped jeans, her love of Chicken McNuggets and dislike of "fancy" restaurants. She never covered up her tattoo —just the opposite. She used it to start conversations, whether with museum visitors or food servers at restaurants, with flight attendants or fellow travelers seated next to her. There was never a time in her life when she didn't think it appropriate to tell people that she was an Auschwitz survivor and that she had forgiven the Nazis. Her fierce protection of her right to be who she was and do what she believed in underlay all of her accomplishments, as she continued to speak about the Holocaust and her forgiveness of the Nazis, even as she experienced backlash. Her authenticity was another quality that endeared her to others, especially young people.

Perhaps the most unexpected thing about Eva was her sense of humor. Eva was a naturally funny person, sometimes for just being so Eva, but often with a purpose. The Holocaust is a very dark subject, difficult to discuss in any circumstances. As with her clothing, she used humor to help people relax, to make it easier to ask questions, to have a conversation, letting people know she was comfortable sharing the details of both the difficult and the happy aspects of her life.

Alex Kor, Eva's son, has many stories about his mom's sense of humor. In 1984, Eva decided to visit Auschwitz by herself. The family was very concerned for her safety on that long trip. Eva went anyway, everything went fine, and she had sweatshirts made for Alex and his sister, Rina. On the front of the sweatshirts was the liberation picture of Eva and Miriam, and on the back it said, "My mom survived Auschwitz and all I got was this lousy sweatshirt."

On the fiftieth anniversary of liberation, Eva was leading a group of people to visit Auschwitz, and Alex joined the group. On arrival, Eva was told the camp wasn't going to let her in because she didn't have the paperwork necessary for the tour bus. She marched to the front of the bus, pulled up her sleeve, pointed to her tattoo, and said, "Fifty years ago, you wouldn't let me out. And now you won't let me in?" They got in that day.

How could an Auschwitz survivor make jokes about the Holocaust? By being a survivor who forgave everyone who had hurt her, healing her own unfathomable emotional pain. According to the accounts of Terre Haute residents, Eva was an angry and bitter woman before she forgave; all agreed that she seemed to be a very different person afterward.

Eva began leading visits to Auschwitz in 1985 and continued to do so until the end of her life. It is impossible to fully prepare to tour Auschwitz; it is a mentally and emotionally grueling, though profound, experience. And while Eva gave it all the weight and darkness it deserves, she never let tour members stay in that deep, dark hole. "Why are you crying?" she would ask a group member in tears. "I'm not crying. I am alive and happy. Your job is to learn what happened here and to be a witness, to make the world a better place when you go home. That is how you respond to the knowledge and insight you have gained here. You don't need to cry."

Indeed, her right to be a victorious survivor rather than a suffering victim was always front and center at Auschwitz. In the summer of 2007, a tourist in Block 6 in Auschwitz confronted Eva and members of her tour group who were taking pictures of Eva with her image from the 1945 liberation photo, which is displayed on a wall. The tourist declared, "This is not appropriate. You shouldn't be laughing, taking pictures, smiling." Eva immediately pointed to herself and said, "That little girl is me, and I've earned the right to smile." By the end of the exchange, the tourist was smiling and crying, which earned her further admonishment from Eva, accompanied by a hug.

Eva embraced joy in many ways, from the simple pleasures of witnessing budding trees in the spring, seeing family and friends, to her daily work at the museum. Her joy also included some mischievousness, as seen when she was in Albuquerque for a teachers' conference. A just-married couple were having their photographs taken in the hotel hallway. Eva saw it as an opportunity to photobomb the shoot while wearing a bowler hat and a mustache she "borrowed" from the photographer's props. During the making of a documentary on her life, Eva and the crew took a trip to Israel, during which the group decided to take an impromptu trip to the Dead Sea. Everyone but Eva had brought shorts or swimwear, but that was not going to be a problem. She waded out into the water in her blue pantsuit, floating in the sea, and loving every minute of it. The little woman had style.

The last years of Eva's life had many other joys. One of the biggest was a documentary, *Eva: A-7063*, released in 2018 and produced by the Indianapolis PBS station, WFYI, and Ted Green Films. It offers important context to Eva's story, particularly during the middle years of her life, when she struggled with anger, bitterness, and rejection. The film was shown on PBS stations across the United States and in Germany, won numerous awards, and has been widely used by teachers, along with her book. Another special friendship bloomed when Scottish musician Raymond Meade read Eva's story and contacted her. The BBC produced a documentary about Eva's story and their friendship.

Because Eva had not always been treated well in her home state, especially in her early years, Eva was especially proud when she was bestowed with the highest honor given to an Indiana citizen, the Sachem Award, by Governor Eric Holcomb. However, in her acceptance speech she revealed bigger political ambition. She wanted to address Congress in Washington, DC, so she could give them a good telling off, and insist they stop bickering and get some things done. She was convinced that she could set those politicians straight.

More recognition came when Eva was asked to participate in a Shoah Foundation project. The exhibit includes hologram-like technology that enables people to interact in question-and-answer form with 3D videos of a survivor. Creating her testimony required Eva to sit inside a room for an entire week with hundreds of lights shining on her, surrounded by cameras, answering over a thousand questions about the various aspects of her life. The recorded testimonies of the survivors can be found in several Holocaust museums in the country, in addition to the Shoah Foundation in Los Angeles.

Eva also received an award from the Anti-Defamation League at the John F. Kennedy Center in Washington, DC, for her efforts in Holocaust education. Though Eva continued to share her story and her message of forgiveness knowing many did not agree with her, she had always hoped for acceptance from the Jewish and Holocaust communities. Her only annoyance at the Kennedy Center award was the five-minute limit on her speech. Getting Eva to speak was easy; sometimes getting her to stop was not.

Eva's thoughts were broad and deep until the end of her life. Her lectures continued to lengthen, because the "life lessons" she wanted to teach young people continued to multiply. And her interests broadened—

she didn't just challenge others to continue thinking of how to make their world a better place, it was a constant process for her, particularly helping young people. She wanted traumatized kids and young adults to have a chance to live on a farm as she did in Israel, healed by the community and the work of gardening and taking care of animals. At school events, she never failed to insist that school uniforms should be worn by all kids— they would look nicer and would prevent students from being judged, for good or bad, on their clothing. The importance she placed on clothing was evident in many situations, perhaps stemming from the warm memories of her mother's care for what her daughters wore.

Eva Mozes Kor died in the early morning hours of July 4, 2019. She had expressed many times that she wanted to live to 110 to be present at the 100th anniversary commemoration event for the Auschwitz liberation. While she was eighty-five and had health issues that had put her in the hospital several times in 2019, she was still going, traveling the world, giving lectures, doing the guided tours, accepting awards, working away in the office in her museum. And if ever there was someone who could survive by sheer determination, it was Eva Kor.

On the Auschwitz group trips that summer, she had been happy and doing well, guiding the museum groups, with nothing to indicate she was in the last days of her life. She tweeted out her delight in finding her favorite food nearby: "Can you believe that today I can get Chicken McNuggets near Auschwitz? That would have been wonderful seventy-five years ago. They taste the same in every country and were delicious." Her death was sudden and unexpected at that point, and there were many people, with her and around the world, who were devastated by her loss. The media coverage was extensive.

In a way it was fitting that Eva died on the Fourth of July. She represented the promise and diversity in immigrants, how they can enrich our lives and our culture in ways we might not expect. As with many immigrants, she was fiercely proud to be an American citizen. She had worked to get her citizenship, and was appreciative of American freedoms and culture. While it was Soviet soldiers who liberated Auschwitz, she always spoke of seeing planes with an American flag on them that gave her hope and how, even then, she associated the American flag with freedom.

The fact that she died in Kraków, the city closest to Auschwitz, was troubling to some. They thought it tragic that she would die there, after braving so much to survive when she was a child. On the other hand, there were fitting aspects of the place of her death. To Eva, Auschwitz was a place of triumph, the biggest of her life. She, a small child, had beaten the Nazis. As she always said, "The Nazis are dead. I am alive." Indeed, it was noticeable to others that she almost seemed the most alive and happy when visiting the camp. In a way, she celebrated her life each time she returned. But those trips were not without dark moments. Eva always laid flowers and lit a candle in honor of her family at the camp, and it was still emotional for her all those years later. The loss of her mother, in particular, was a pain that never completely went away.

Eva Kor, the humanitarian, the fighter for justice, for healing, for peace, was in a way formed in that camp, a woman of strength and single-minded determination. While for much of her life she did not believe in God—which is very common among Holocaust survivors—her views had changed in the years before her death. She expressed to several that she thought God could exist and perhaps she was meant to go through what she did, and to discover the healing power of forgiveness and spread that message around the world.

The last day of her life, she was just outside the Auschwitz grounds. A boys choir was visiting the camp and heard she was going to be there. The trip coordinator and close friend, Beth Nairn, sent Eva a text message, telling her that thirty-six handsome young men were waiting to see her and wanted to sing for her. Eva arrived a few minutes later and requested her favorite song, "The Impossible Dream," the lyrics expressing her belief that anything is possible. Somehow, the choir director and boys found the words and sang a bit followed by two other beautiful songs they had rehearsed, and she thoroughly enjoyed their performance.

Eva also had plans to visit the Katowice convent for the first time since her stay there after liberation, but alas, that was not to be. Staff of her museum had visited a few days beforehand to verify the location before taking Eva on the trip. In an incredible coincidence, the nuns wore habits, currently and in 1945, of the same bright blue she had adopted as her color later in life. On seeing photographs of the nuns, she agreed that the blue she loved might have been a forgotten association with freedom and safety. She also met Rabbi Bleich, Vice President of the Jewish World Congress. When Eva explained her forgiveness, he asked her if she had forgiven only on her own behalf or for others. She assured him that she had only forgiven on her own behalf, and he told her he thought her forgiveness was fine. She declared that she liked him.

She died in the early-morning hours of July 4, having had a prominent Jewish rabbi give his blessing on her forgiveness, a personal performance by a boys choir, and doing what she loved most—leading the group through Auschwitz, telling her story, feeling gratitude and joy, and sharing her message of forgiveness to heal the world.

When the documentary maker Ted Green had asked Governor Holcomb to envision the scene if ever Eva had her wish and was invited to speak to Congress, he said, "Well, there would be one giant in the room, and it would be Eva." Without a doubt, she was one of the giant of our times.

Eva used to tell children and teens that they had the power to change the world. She understood that people, young and old, think they have to be part of a big organization to make change on a broad scale. But what Eva taught us, by words and deed, is the power of the individual.

If a four-foot-nine Auschwitz survivor, orphan, refugee, immigrant, realtor with a Romanian accent in Terre Haute, Indiana, can find a worldwide audience for her story and her message, any one of us can make a difference, whoever and wherever we are.

Eva always ended her lectures, "Anger is a seed for war; forgiveness is a seed for peace." I hope readers will be inspired to choose peace, in honor of the one, and surely the only, Eva Mozes Kor.

AUTHOR'S NOTE

Lisa Rojany Buccieri, April 2009

This book came about through the efforts of many people. First and foremost, it is based on one person's memory. Eva Mozes Kor is an eyewitness to a multitude of crimes against humanity. Through her lectures at schools and in the Holocaust museum she founded, Eva always knew that her story was an important one for young people to learn. When Peggy Tierney first approached her about publishing a book, she agreed immediately. Eva's greatest dream was that her book would be used in schools to teach young people about the Holocaust and be inspired to use its lessons in their own lives.

Katie McKy interviewed Eva extensively, asking many pertinent questions and getting Eva to open up and express herself in ways that readers could relate to.

Susan Goldman Rubin wrote an extensive, detailed outline, both meeting Eva in person and adding much valuable, insightful research to the materials drawn from. Without Susan, the writing of this book would not have been possible in the short time allotted.

Peggy Tierney, our editor at Tanglewood Books, served as Eva's cheerleader for years through several writers and too many drafts to count. She knew Eva had an important story to tell, and she believed that it needed to be told. I want to thank Peggy for believing in my ability to take these materials and write this book in a way that both adheres to the truth as Eva recalled it and also brings her story to life so that young readers can relive it in the safety of these pages. I can only hope that those readers find this book worth all our efforts.

It was my privilege to work on this important project, helping to pass on Eva Mozes Kor's story to a new generation of readers. There are not many children of the Holocaust, much less many of the Mengele twins, who lived to tell their stories. Eva did. And this story is told in her voice, in the first person, as an adult looking back over sixty-five years, to a time when a little girl, clutching the trembling hand of her identical twin sister, showed up at the gates of horror—and survived.

AUTHOR BIOGRAPHIES

EVA MOZES KOR (1939–2019) founded an organization for surviving Mengele twins in 1985, and helped to pressure governments to search for Josef Mengele. In 1995, she opened a small Holocaust museum in Terre Haute, Indiana, which grew into the CANDLES Holocaust Museum and Education Center, at which she gave presentations and tours, especially to school-aged children. She was a recognized speaker, both nationally and internationally, on topics related to the Holocaust, medical ethics, forgiveness, and peace. She was covered in numerous media outlets, including *60 Minutes* and *20/20*, and was the subject of a documentary, *Forgiving Dr. Mengele*. The website for the museum is www.candlesholocaustmuseum.org

LISA ROJANY BUCCIERI has written over one hundred children's books, including several award-winning and bestselling titles. She is also a publishing executive and editor with over thirty years of experience in the industry, and is the lead writer for *Writing Children's Books for Dummies*. As well as spearheading four publishing startups, Lisa has simultaneously run her own business, Editorial Services of L.A. She has been Editorial/Publishing Director for Golden Books, Price Stern Sloan/Penguin Group USA, Intervisual Books, Gateway Learning Corp (Hooked on Phonics), and Intervisual Books. Lisa lives with her family in Los Angeles.

PICTURE CREDITS

Page 76: Courtesy of State Museum Auschwitz-Birkenau in Oświęcim, Poland.

Page 79: A photograph taken of an original document in State Museum Auschwitz-Birkenau archives, from Eva Kor's private collection.

Page 80: Photograph of document from Eva Kor's private collection.

Page 135: Courtesy of State Museum Auschwitz-Birkenau in Oświęcim, Poland.

Page 147: Courtesy of the United States Holocaust Memorial Museum.

Page 153: From Eva Kor's private collection.

Page 162: From Eva Kor's private collection.

Page 168: From Eva Kor's private collection.

Page 176: From Eva Kor's private collection.

Page 179: From Eva Kor's private collection.

Page 180: From Eva Kor's private collection.

Page 183: From Eva Kor's private collection.

The views or opinions expressed in this book, and the context in which the images are used, do not necessarily reflect the views or policy of, nor imply approval or endorsement by, the United States Holocaust Memorial Museum.

ADDITIONAL RESOURCES

Learn more about the documentary
and related materials at:
www.thestoryofeva.com

Visit Eva's museum online:
www.candlesholocaustmuseum.org